All
the Presidents'
Pets

All
the Presidents'
Pets

The Inside Story of One Reporter
Who Refused to Roll Over

Mo Rocca

Crown Publishers
New York

Photograph credits appear on pages 237–238.

Published by Crown Publishers, New York, New York.
Member of the Crown Publishing Group, a division of Random House, Inc.
www.crownpublishing.com

CROWN is a trademark and the Crown colophon is a registered trademark of Random House, Inc.

Printed in the United States of America

DESIGN BY ELINA D. NUDELMAN

Library of Congress Cataloging-in-Publication Data
Rocca, Mo.
All the presidents' pets: the story of one reporter who refused to roll over / Mo Rocca.—1st ed.   1. United States—Politics and government—Humor.
2. Reporters and reporting—United States—Humor.   3. American wit and humor.   I. Title.
PN6231.P6R58   2004
818'.602—dc22   2004010505

ISBN 1-4000-5225-4

10 9 8 7 6 5 4 3 2 1

First Edition

For Pop and Mamita

Contents

Contents

CONTENTS

White House Press Briefing

APRIL 1, 2004

PRESS SECRETARY SCOTT McCLELLAN: Helen, go ahead.

HELEN THOMAS: When is the President going to hold a news conference? He has not tackled any of these issues in an overall news conference, full-scale, since last December 15th. Isn't it about time that we had a time—chance, that is, to question?

SCOTT: I appreciate your question, and I always try to work to accommodate your needs.

HELEN: Well, is there any possibility of having one—

SCOTT: Well, there's nothing I'm announcing today. But I understand your question and I will certainly take it into consideration.

HELEN: Is it a difficult question?

. . .

2ND REPORTER: A couple things. First, I just wanted to associate myself with Helen's request here. There are a lot—

SCOTT: Anybody else? Anybody? Okay.

2ND REPORTER: It would be great to hear from the President.

SCOTT: Okay, we will do one later today. Oh, April Fool's, I'm sorry.

Prologue

The remarkable thing about Daniel Chester French's sculpture of a seated Abraham Lincoln is the way it captures both the sixteenth President's godliness and his humanness. Lincoln, the former rail splitter with almost no formal schooling, is memorialized in a nineteen-foot-high statue of Georgia white marble and seated inside a Greek temple—a fitting tribute to the man who saved, then died for, our democracy.

And yet he is totally approachable, even kindly, not aloof like Jefferson or inscrutable like Washington. The statue may be colossal but the expression is undeniably human—worn and pensive, eyes cast downward, modeled after Mathew Brady's photographs.

Lincoln has always been both a leader of irreproachable principle and at the same time eminently reasonable, political in the best sense of the word. He compromised, even wheeled and dealed, for an uncompromisingly noble goal—the survival of America. Lincoln was strong because he could bend, like the mature branch of a willow tree. Today's so-called ideologue is ineffectual, a brittle twig.

Surrounding the President, etched on the north and south

walls of the Lincoln Memorial, are the Gettysburg Address and my personal favorite, the second inaugural speech. "With malice toward none; with charity for all," Lincoln urges us to strive on to finish the work we are in—with firmness, yes, but always with compassion.

Which is why the sight of my body floating facedown at the western end of the Reflecting Pool, just a few yards from the bottom step of the Lincoln Memorial, my hand still clutching a faded Pinocchio chew toy, would have saddened him so deeply.

How did I, a thirtysomething journalist on a simple quest to save our once again imperiled democracy, get to this point? Only recently had I discovered the White House's deepest darkest secret. Now everything was hanging in the balance.

My story begins three and a half weeks before I ended up so unceremoniously in the water. And just like any story that's equal parts *All the President's Men* and *Charlotte's Web* (with a little *Da Vinci Code* thrown in), it's a tale that must be told—even if I never get invited back to the White House Correspondents Dinner.

1

Strangeness on a Train

All aboard!

The Acela Express between Washington and New York launched its maiden voyage in the fall of 2000 as a high-speed alternative to the poky, college-student-infested Amtrak train. With their double-espressos, laptops, and *New York Times* in hand, politicians, lobbyists, newscasters, and pundits flocked to the express service like it was the Concorde in its heyday, praising its ease and speed. Forget about the Delta Shuttle. After 9/11 no one was allowed to walk through the aisles once the plane was in the air, so it was impossible to network.

Because of its state-of-the-art everything (outlets at every seat!), the silver-and-turquoise bullet train quickly became a schmoozefest on wheels, a veritable kissass-ela. "It's so European!" gushed GOP leader-turned-lobbyist Dick Armey to Massachusetts Democrat Barney Frank. Across from them in a four-seater, columnist Tina Brown fawned over freshman congressman Ryan Seacrest. "How *do* you do it all?" she asked him. And in between cars, leggy conservative pundette Laura Ingraham canoodled in the shadows with pint-sized Clinton cabinet secretary Robert Reich—strange bedfellows indeed but on the Acela they shared one important trait: these powerbrokers were all arriving in Washington a full fifteen minutes faster than the lowly schmucks stuck on the Metroliner.

The Acela was especially busy the last time I took it. I wasn't en route to an assignment, though. My trip *was* the assignment, part of my current gig on MSNBC, also known as the Michelle Kwan of the twenty-four-hour cable news channels. (No matter how hard it tried, it always seemed to land on its ass.)

I wore a fake mustache and took my position behind the counter of the café car. It was the latest in my series of undercover reports focusing on different service jobs, appropriately called "Pressure"—and appropriately accompanied by the Billy Joel song "Pressure," or, as the singer pronounced it, "Preshah!" Each segment featured me thrown into a different job, wearing a different disguise each time. As a furniture mover I got to wear a soul patch. As a mohel I wore *payos.*

The segment was part of MSNBC's latest experiment in prime-time news, *Hard Time with Jim Traficant,* starring the flamboyant former Ohio congressman and convict with the Davy Crockett hairpiece. From prison Jim had seen me on TV and become a fan. When MSNBC approached him, he demanded I join the ensemble. "You get me that Mo. He works my funny-bone real good."

Unfortunately *Hard Time* was scheduled against the mighty Bill O'Reilly. If O'Reilly and his two million viewers occupied a no-spin zone at the nucleus of cable news, we were a negatively charged speck in the outermost valence shell.

This was hardly the kind of work I envisioned when as a boy I dreamed of covering presidential politics. It was humbling, to say the least. (Only moments earlier C-SPAN's Brian Lamb had gone ballistic on me for overheating his Sara Lee cheese Danish. "You're supposed to poke a hole in the plastic before you nuke it, retard!" he shouted.) To make matters worse I was saddled with a 315-pound cameraman named Phil, who spent most of the day on his cell phone prattling on with his fellow conspiracy theorists: "It's absolutely true, Norma. The first President Bush and several Bin Ladens once went to hear cabaret singer Bobby Short . . . at New York's *Carlyle* Hotel. You can't make this stuff up." If I tried to get sharp with him, he only threw it back in my face, reminding me of his own glory days. "When Morley interviewed Betty Ford, guess who did the light-meter reading," he gloated.

But like it or not, Phil was my cameraman, and I needed his cooperation if I was ever going to prove that I was worthy of a meatier assignment. I picked up a copy of the *Washington Post* I'd been keeping behind the counter. "Hey, Phil, did you know that Amtrak requested $1.82 billion in federal assistance last year?"

Phil didn't hear me. He was polishing off a pack of peanut M&M's and staring at the café car TV, which was tuned to CNN.

Earlier that day, President Bush had once again dropped his dog Barney, this time at a gathering of Hispanic businesswomen. (It had happened once before, at an airfield in Waco.) It didn't seem like a particularly remarkable event—and playing it over and over didn't make it more so. In fact the only thing that was remotely interesting was the split-second startled look on Bush's face *before* he dropped the Scottie. But Phil didn't notice that.

"Poor doggie," he whimpered. I tried again to get his attention.

"So anyway, Amtrak requested over $1.8 billion and yet its on-time record continued to decline."

"And?" Phil snapped without looking at me.

"And that's pretty outrageous," I said defensively. "This is the story we should look into." Phil finally turned to me with a look one-quarter compassionate, three-quarters belittling that read, "You sad deluded clown. You really think they want you to be a real reporter?" But before I could respond, a woman's voice piped in.

The first strike in the War on Terriers?

"*And* yet it's still faster than the shuttle door to door. How are you, cutie?" My cover was blown, by none other than CBS's Lesley Stahl, a former network "colleague."

"Hey, Les," I said, forcing a casual smile, then remembering it was no use pretending I wasn't embarrassed. I was wearing a fake mustache.

"Don't you 'Hey, Les' me, Mr. Adorable Café Club Car Undercover Agent, you! Give me a hug!!" I awkwardly hugged Lesley over the counter. "I'd kiss you but your sexy *Magnum, P.I.*

mustache might burn me! And, Phil, what on earth are you doing shooting for CABLE?!" The way she shrieked "cable" made me want to put my head in the microwave.

Phil seized the chance to take a swipe at me. "Helping the needy," he sneered.

Lesley threw her head back with a laugh. "We really miss you at the network, honey," she said to me, grabbing my hand. She couldn't resist adding, "But cable allows you to focus on *hard* news. No fluff here." She and Phil both cackled.

There was no denying I looked silly. Then again, Lesley was wearing a pink leather jacket, miniskirt, and spike heels. Was she off to cover a rumble between the Sharks and the Jets?

"So what's going on in D.C.?" Phil asked her, hoping that she might sweep him off to an interview with some visiting head of state.

"The anniversary of Chandra Levy's disappearance," she said, suddenly somber.

"*60 Minutes?*" Phil asked.

Lesley quickly changed the subject—she must have been shooting for *48 Hours*. She looked up at the menu. "Mo, sweetie, tell me about this Maine lobster wrap 'enhanced with lemon mustard aioli, complemented by crisp cabbage slaw.' Very fancy-sounding." By the time she finished reading she was leaning almost over the counter, one leg, bent at the knee, sexily kicked up behind her.

"Well, let's see," I said, fumbling with one of the sandwiches. "It looks like the lobster is wrapped in some sort of a fennel tortilla with—"

"Why am I asking you?" she kidded, grabbing my collar and pulling my ear right up to her lips. "You're not a food reporter, Maurice," she cooed, using my birth name. "You're an *investigative* reporter!" I'd just about had it with Lesley's Mrs. Robinson routine when her cell phone rang and she pushed me away to grab it. "It's Andrew calling! Must be important." She wanted me to believe it was CBS News president Andrew Heyward, but of course I knew it was Andy Rooney. She covered the phone for a second. "Sorry, boys, but I have to take this. It's the *network*." And she was gone in an instant, the clicking of her heels receding down the aisle of the café car.

"Isn't she amazing?" Phil said dreamily.

"Amazing," I said, through clenched teeth.

2

Some Background on How I Became Jim Traficant's Bitch

Maybe I was overly sensitive to taunts from network people. After all I'd once been at network, before I "transitioned" to cable.

For years I'd dutifully filed quirky reports for the CBS *Early Show,* which every TV critic described as "the long-suffering *Early Show.*" (Most of those writers had assigned the phrase its own F-key.) My beat included everything from a behind-the-scenes look at *Survivor: East Timor* to a whatever-happened-to look at the contestants from *Survivor: Chechnya.*

When our executive producer forced me to serve as an usher for the *Early Show*'s on-air wedding—in which the groom had been married once before on NBC's *Today*—I knew it was time to leave.

The ratings were one problem. One week, when *Today* was in Los Angeles and ABC's *Good Morning America* was in London, we pulled out all the stops. Cohosts Harry Smith, Hannah Storm, Julie Chen, and René Syler—"Harry and his harem," the crew used to snicker—and I put on grass skirts and brandished tiki torches for our own game of *Survivor: Early Show.* But the only person who stopped to look through the windows of our street-side plaza was a homeless man with no pants.

11

Worse still, our ratings actually dropped when the five of us underwent simultaneous colonoscopies.

More important, I wanted to be a political reporter. I looked at Jeff Greenfield, the brainiac who left ABC's *Nightline* for CNN so that he could do even more hard news. The network-for-cable gamble had paid off for him. Why not me? Yes, MSNBC was in fourth place among the three main twenty-four-hour news channels (Nielsen stood by its figures), but it was better than Oxygen, the only other cable outlet that gave me an offer. And so, in a very small way, I was on my way.

My goal was, had been for a long time, to cover the White House—the big kahuna among political assignments. Since childhood I'd had a deep, even romantic, fascination with all things presidential. (More on that later.) MSNBC's then-president Eric Sorenson wouldn't promise me that primo beat right off the bat. "We're in a state of flux right now," he explained. "But don't worry, we're in the Mo Rocca business for the long haul."

When I signed my contract, though, Eric surprised me—but not with the White House. "We want to try something alternative with you, Mo." I was a funny guy, he said, and that could play with a younger demographic. "MSNBC's mission from the beginning has been to harness the current-events curiosity of young, hip viewers. That means being serious and sexy and not talking down to them." The only thing vaguely sexy about that so-called mission statement was the word "harness," but I was intrigued. Eric continued: "Our studies have shown that Generation Z is hungry for news, but they just don't trust the 'three wise men'— you know, Tom, Dan, and Peter. You can be an ambassador, Mo." I was bewildered but flattered, too, by the notion that I could be a bridge to disaffected hipsters everywhere.

Thus was born MSNBC's *Rocca Your World,* a platform for me to ask the questions of politicians and lobbyists that everyone wanted to ask but wouldn't. I would be the television journalism world's id.

To run the show MSNBC brought in a twenty-five-year-old former production assistant from HBO's acclaimed *Da Ali G Show*. Everyone was duly impressed by Seamus. He had never finished college, he played the drums in his own jam band, *and* he'd once been named as a defendant in an online music-file-sharing suit. "This guy's really in touch," said Eric knowingly.

Tall and lanky, with a tousled head of red hair, uniformed in brown Wrangler cords, a Willy Wonka T-shirt that was three sizes too small, and a pair of Vans on his feet, Seamus looked like he'd skateboarded right off a *Vice* magazine shoot. Every time he skidded into our studio in Secaucus, New Jersey, a frisson of excitement whipped through the newsroom. "We're going to take your grandpop's newscast and flip it inside out, Moises," Seamus decreed. "Kids will dig it because they'll know you're winking at 'em the whole time. Solid?"

I wasn't. But I didn't want to be difficult, so when Seamus decided I needed a new look, I went along. I stopped cutting, washing, or combing my hair and borrowed money from my parents to buy a Juicy brand velour track suit and a pair of Chuck Taylor All-Stars. Seamus even convinced me to get "Murrow" tattooed on my left shoulder. But when the two of us came back with blue-tinted Samuel L. Jackson frames for me, Eric overruled us. "The look may be cool, Seamus, but the audience has got to see his eyes. Standards and practices."

Seamus put his arm around me and confided, "Execs need to feel like they're part of the creative process. Let's say we give ground on this one, Mo-meister, aiiight den?" Uh, sure. It's not like we had a choice. Eric suggested we call former MSNBC correspondent Ashleigh Banfield, famous for her sexy eyewear, for another direction on specs. I'd never actually met Ashleigh, but Seamus had once made out with her at a Radiohead concert, so he did the talking.

Ashleigh was now reporting for ANN, the Arctic News Network. For the past two months she'd been busy reporting on preparations for Alaska's Iditarod sled dog race. After that she was scheduled to spend another two months covering potential Iditarod fallout, before gearing up to report on next year's Iditarod. Somehow she found time to take Seamus's call.

She referred us to Selima Optique, a pricey eyeglasses shop in SoHo. Within days I was sporting a pair of chunky electric green ultra-Teutonic frames, trendier than anything architect Daniel Libeskind could dream up.

I was undeniably stylin', and yet I just didn't feel like me. But Seamus was absolutely confident. My first guest was Republican rocker Ted Nugent. He and I were to debate gun control as we played with G.I. Joes. "Right out of the gates we're going way post-ironic," said Seamus during our prep.

It went surprisingly well. During the segment Nugent got so carried away making his own artillery sounds that viewers must have at the very least been mystified. I asked Seamus if I'd handled it okay. "Fo' shizzle, my nizzle!" he exclaimed in his best wigger voice. He wrapped his arm around my neck and gave me a noogie. When NBC News president Neal Shapiro called to say he was "amused"—in retrospect, I think he said "bemused"—a cheer went up in the studio. (In fairness to Neal, we spent little time talking about gun control. Seamus felt that that would have been too obvious.)

After the show Seamus brought the whole staff out for a round of Schlitz. (Pabst Blue Ribbon, or PBR, was "yesterday's hip shitty beer," he said.) He even convinced Eric to wear his trucker cap that night, though by that time trucker hats were over—again—so Seamus was really just setting Eric up.

It was all pretty heady. For the first time in sixteen years I shot-gunned a beer. I also smoked my very first American Spirit cigarette. Seamus dubbed me "Mo King"—not terribly clever, but we were all so happy we laughed anyway. MSNBC might have a new hit on its slate. That night Seamus sucked face with one of our newsreaders in the bar, even though he said he was dating actress Gina Gershon.

Eric immediately capitalized on this success and got me booked as one of the sassy talking heads on VH1's newest list show, *VH1's 35 Funniest Brunettes.* Was Courteney Cox (#5) really funnier than Joan Cusack (#9)? I didn't think so but I did my snarky best.

This would be the first of many "Mo Rocca branding" ventures, Eric promised. MSNBC's *Mo Rocca the Vote* would inevitably spin off in time for the next presidential election. "You'll make Anderson Cooper wish he'd never left *The Mole,*" gloated Eric.

It was undeniably exciting. I began Googling myself, first once a day, then once every hour or so. Oh my God, I was stalked twice on Gawker in one week! Then Seamus asked one of the MSNBC interns he'd slept with to set up a Yahoo! fan club for me. After two weeks there were still only twelve members, all teenage girls. I hung on every word they typed. Roccandroll43 was the most prolific: "Mo is so pale, skinny, and uncomfortable with himself. It's adorable!"

But any momentum I might enjoy as a "personality" still depended largely on the success of the show. And alas, the Nugent experience turned out to be a lone bright spot for *Rocca Your World.* Before the month was finished, the political establishment quickly cooled to what Seamus had coined our "anti-newscast."

"Why am I asking James Baker to play Twister with me?" I asked Seamus before one taping.

"Because you're tweaking the whole former-secretary-of-state convention. The kids'll love it."

"That doesn't make any sense."

"The line between what's real and what's not, we're fucking with it. It's satire." Seamus was becoming less friendly, more agitated. "Bro, you're overthinking it. Sometimes it's just funny."

Secretary Baker not so graciously declined my invitation, as did most of Washington's powerbrokers past and present. Even Pennsylvania senator Arlen Specter, who had recently shown up on Jay Leno's *Tonight Show* in full clown makeup (he was getting ready for a presidential run in 2008), turned us down.

That's when viewers started fleeing in droves, and the critics smelled blood. The *Washington Post*'s Tom Shales wrote that "Rocca is ten minutes past his fifteen minutes of fame" and that I "deserved to die." The *New York Times*'s Frank Rich served me with the harshest indictment of all: *"Rocca Your World* made me cry more than the recent revival of *Gypsy,* and for all the wrong reasons."

By this time Seamus had become bored—he had already "embedded" every woman at the network—and announced that he was moving on to direct a production of *Macbeth* with meth-addicted McDonaldland characters on the Lower East Side.

"We're not connecting here, Mochise. You guys are way too linear."

Rather than bring in someone to fix the show, the network started eating into my hour. First came extended weather breaks. Then they forced me to make room for "Imus moments," during which the I-Man was usually blasting away at my show. (Imus was implacable. He returned every check I wrote to his charity ranch.)

I was no safer in cyberspace. On AmIAnnoying.com, I discovered that according to voters I was more annoying than Pia Zadora and only slightly less annoying than Jeffrey Dahmer. My Yahoo! fan site had already shuttered, after the lone remaining member, Roccandroll43, wrote, "Mo is so pale, skinny, and uncomfortable with himself. It really grosses me out."

What hurt most of all, though, was the treatment I got from Washington's normally good-natured political comedy song-and-dance troupe, the Capitol Steps. Their latest revue, *Please, No Mo*

Rocca included the biting "You're the Flop" (sung to the melody of Cole Porter's "You're the Top"), which soon became an even bigger hit than last season's "Bomb Bomb Iraq" (sung to the melody of the Beach Boys' "Barbara Ann"). The lyrics were scathing:

> *You're the Flop*
> *You're as funny as Cheney*
> *You're the Flop*
> *But not nearly as zany*
>
> *You're worse than watching roll call on C-SPAN*
> *You're a filibuster*
> *Without the luster*
> *You deserve the can!*

That's when Eric pulled the plug on *Rocca Your World* and conceived my "Pressure" segment. "Look, Mo, we might have pushed you too far away from your roots. This will be a much better fit," Eric said.

"But I came to cable to avoid things like wearing silly disguises."

"Hey, there's nothing silly about the proud men and women who work in America's service industries," he said a little self-righteously. "Besides, Jim likes you."

Hard Time with Jim Traficant, featuring my "Pressure" segment, would premiere only days later. Traficant had been out of prison for two months when the network snatched him up. Besides my participation, he demanded that he be allowed to wear his orange prison jumpsuit on camera and that Gary Condit be the first guest. (Condit was the only member who voted against Jim's expulsion from the House of Representatives.) The network had high hopes.

I didn't have much choice but to submit to Traficant, so I packed my bags and moved down to D.C., the town where I grew up and where the show was being taped.

Back in the café car, stinging from Lesley Stahl's barbs, I sucked it up and committed myself to soldiering onward. Phil was still watching Bush dropping Barney—from three news angles now and with on-air analysis from Bill Schneider.

"So, Phil," I said optimistically, "I figured since we're here, we may as well get a few sound bites from the conductor on the status of the split in the track outside Metropark. It could become a big story."

Phil shot me a look of unalloyed contempt. I whimpered.

3

There's Something About Harry

(AND ALL OUR OTHER PRESIDENTS)

The only good part about being back in Washington was that I'd be near the White House. And the White House is where the President lives. Allow me to digress for a moment . . .

The President. The Commander-in-Chief. The Chief Executive. POTUS. Maybe I was fascinated by the office because I'd been raised in D.C., a mill town like L.A., where the President was the undisputed number-one star. Other kids might have become blasé but not I. Staring at the White House was magical, like looking through the gates of Paramount Studios.

It seemed that the office had worked a kind of alchemy on all its forty-two occupants. (George W. Bush is the forty-third President because Grover Cleveland's nonconsecutive terms are counted twice.) In each case, the presidency took a man who seemed ordinary and transformed him into something more. Silent Cal Coolidge was no longer boring; he was stoic. Taft was no longer fat; he was robust. Clinton was no longer an adulterer; he was popular with women voters. Even George Washington, already a god among men, grew still larger than life in office. Had he never been President, he would have still been "First in War," maybe even "First in the Hearts of his Countrymen." But without the "First in Peace" part, the whole quote would have fallen apart.

Cynics believed that a presidential mythmaking machine was at work, serving the American public's need, in the absence of royalty, to believe, say, that Warren Harding was a 1920s Abe Lincoln. (Warren Harding did have the biggest feet of any president—size fourteen and a half. That has to count for something.) They believed that the White House press corps aided and abetted this myth.

Perhaps it was no coincidence that the first modern all-powerful President, Teddy Roosevelt, had an especially close relationship with reporters and gave them their first pressroom inside the White House. He did this, the skeptics claimed, so that he could manage the flow of information more easily and control the way the American people perceived him.

But honestly, could anyone deny that TR *was* nearly superhuman? Through a hail of bullets this former asthmatic ran all the way up Cuba's Kettle Hill without stopping for breath. (That's right, Kettle Hill. San Juan Hill gets all the credit, but it was a lot less important.) This was no whitewashing.

Sure, the press might have been tricked or bullied by the White House on occasion. In *The Boys on the Bus,* journalist Timothy Crouse described the Nixon-era White House press corps members as flacks, called them "handout artists." But ever since Watergate, Presidents were picked apart from A to Z, and former Presidents were constantly reassessed. The Starr Report was excessive in book form. Did it really need to be put out as a book on tape? Though I suppose David Ogden Stiers's narration did help class it up.

And still my faith and, yes, awe in the transformative power of the office remained intact. Look at George W. Bush: The *New York Times*'s Frank Bruni, whom the President nicknamed "Panchito," described a likable Bush "ambling" into office in January 2001. Nine months later, and only a week after 9/11,

Bush stood atop the smoldering rubble of Lower Manhattan and rallied the nation. At the time, Bob Woodward (nickname "Woody") compared Bush favorably with FDR. Not long afterward Chris Matthews (nickname "Sugarlips") called him "an easygoing Prince Hal transformed by instinct and circumstance into a warrior King Henry." America (nickname "The Big Enchilada") and I were once again impressed.

Most wondrous of all, anyone could still become President. Ronald Reagan started out life dirt poor. Critics minimized his achievement and said that his status in Hollywood had given him a leg up. Status? *Hellcats of the Navy* should have consigned Ron and Nancy to three years in the brig, minimum. But in America, anyone with Reagan's talent to lead had a shot at becoming President. Sure it helped if you were white, male, and Protestant (or like a Kennedy, Protestant-ish), but there were still a bunch of those.

But it wasn't just the marquee presidents I revered. I had a special fondness for the forgotten Chief Executives.

While some kids were into sports stars, I was into James Buchanan and Franklin Pierce, the Presidents you couldn't remember were actually Presidents. The majority served during a relatively low point in presidential power, between Lincoln and Teddy Roosevelt—disproportionately from Ohio, targets of crazed anarchists, with lots of facial hair. (With his muttonchops, Chester Alan Arthur was hipper than Seamus could ever hope to be.)

My penchant for Presidents big and small found a new outlet when I began visiting presidential homes and gravesites. It was the perfect hobby for someone who'd never had a real hobby. (Memorizing all the world capitals wasn't really a hobby, though things did get sort of hectic after the breakup of the old Soviet Union.)

The visits began about five years ago. I was driving through the Hudson Valley on the way home from visiting my grandmother when I saw a sign for eighth President Martin Van Buren's house in Kinderhook, New York. Lindenwald, as it is known, which is Dutch for "grove of trees," was modeled after a Venetian villa and still had its original Zuber-designed wallpaper depicting vivid scenes of Alsatian stag hunting and wild fowling. My tour guide was a way-too-cool-for-school college student named Sari Van Buren. "Are you related?" I asked. "Uh, yeah," she said, doing her best popular-girl-answering-a-lame-question voice. "And, like, please don't lean on the sideboard. It's a period piece."

Perhaps it was Sari's grossed-out description of her foppish ancestor's Wedgwood china chamber pot, or maybe it was the way she mispronounced *poudreuse*—why the President had his own eighteenth-century French vanity I'll never know—but gradually my hobby became an obsession.

After a trip to the Grover Cleveland birthplace in Caldwell, New Jersey—the collection included a piece of his inaugural fruitcake—I rented a car and headed to the Midwest, land of the forgotten Presidents. At the Benjamin Harrison house in Indianapolis I tagged along with a group of restless fourth-graders led by volunteer Wanda Wheeler, a seventy-five-year-old battleax in a full Victorian gown who sounded exactly like Granny Clampett from *The Beverly Hillbillies*. It was 97 degrees outside and not much cooler inside, and I half expected one of the boys to grab "Little Ben's" flintlock pistol and turn it on Wanda. But Wanda was a lesson in the persuasive power of fanaticism.

"Now LOOK at that Reginaphone!" she barked, pointing to the phonograph's precursor (rhymes with vagina-phone). "Have you ever seen a Reginaphone like that?" she asked. "NO YOU HAVEN'T!" she snapped before anyone could answer. "Now LOOK at that Hoosier kitchen cabinet," she ordered us. "Have you ever seen a Hoosier kitchen cabinet like that? NO YOU HAVEN'T!" In fact I had, at William Henry Harrison's estate in Vincennes—which also had an exquisitely crafted pie safe—but I was afraid to interrupt her.

Visiting with some of my oldest friends. Clockwise from top left: Chester Alan Arthur, William Howard Taft, James Buchanan, and William McKinley.

By the end of the tour the kids were fresh converts to her Benjamin Harrison cult. Forget the critics who had called him a "study in inaction" with a handshake like a "wilted petunia." The kids now understood that the twenty-third President was a virile and fearless leader. It was agreed that the time had come to sandblast Mount Rushmore and replace it with Benjamin Harrison. (As for the boy in the Colts jersey who begged Wanda to let him touch Caroline Harrison's whalebone bristle brush, the change was even more profound.)

Did Wanda go too far? Perhaps. Few scholars would agree that Harrison freed the slaves. But the fact remained that he deserved much more respect than he had been given.

As for the gravesites, it seemed fair that the less ballyhooed Presidents had the more extravagant tombs. Jogging up the 108 steps of the McKinley Memorial I felt like Rocky, though I realize that my jumping and fist-pumping upon reaching our twenty-fifth President's Windsor green granite sarcophagus was wholly inappropriate, and I now offer profuse apologies to the McKinley estate.

When I wasn't visiting homes and gravesites I was reading about everything presidential. Mothers, siblings, cars, major medical operations. (George Washington did not in fact have wooden teeth. Grover Cleveland did have a rubber jaw.) And the First Lady flashcards my grandmother had given me long ago were rarely out of reach.

My colleagues at the *Early Show* took note of my fixations. They suspected that I was suffering from a major First Void in my life.

"I think you need to ask yourself why you're so interested in all these dead guys," anchor Harry Smith counseled me over lunch one day in the CBS commissary.

"Harry, with all due respect, you're the guy who hosts *Biography*."

"I'm concerned, that's all. Besides, many of *Biography*'s subjects are alive."

"So you'd prefer I hang around outside Angie Dickinson's house?" I asked, a bit sarcastically I'm afraid.

"And you wonder why you're not covering the White House for CBS," Harry snapped. "Asshole."

BUT EVEN LOOKING BACK from my current low point, I knew I'd made the right move. I still stood a greater chance of covering the White House for MSNBC than I ever had at CBS. And that made all the difference: Reporters who covered the White House performed a great service to today's public—

and tomorrow's. After all, as *Washington Post* publisher Philip Graham put it, journalism is "the first draft of history." (Yes, someday historians would pore over old issues of *Maxim*.)

As the cab passed the Kennedy Center en route to my apartment, I thought of JFK and how, according to Robert Dallek's recent biography, he'd suffered more than anyone had ever known. I hated physical pain so I counted myself lucky. Gluing on a fake mustache only hurt emotionally—though taking it off did kind of burn.

I just needed to do my job at *Hard Time* with as much diligence and dignity as possible. If there were any justice, I would get that White House assignment eventually. It just wouldn't happen on this particular program. Jim had made that clear.

Only last week, during the show's "Solitary Confinement" segment, during which Jim screamed directly into the camera for five minutes, he declaimed, "Republicans, Democrats, I hate 'em all. We don't have time to talk politics on this show!"

"But, Jim," I ventured during the commercial break as I came onto set to intro my "TCBY Pressure" segment, "this is a news analysis show. Politics is going to come in there somewhere."

Jim laughed and squeezed my neck a little too hard. "You just hush now, little Mo. You're going to keep makin' 'em squeal at home." Then he yelled to the control room, "Now beam me up!"

4

Stepping in Dhue-Dhue

The phone was ringing as I entered my apartment. I'd only been living there for a month and few people had my number, so I figured it was a telemarketer. "Yup," I snapped into the phone.

"Wow. Someone's grumpy. Sorenson here."

"Eric! Sorry about that."

"No worries. I'm the one calling to say sorry. I've got some bad news. *Hard Time*'s been canceled. We just haven't been pulling the numbers."

"You're kidding!" I said, delighted. I instantly reined it in. This was supposed to be bad news. "I'm so sorry, Eric. We've only been on a month and we were doing better in the ratings, I thought. I'm pretty sure we were ahead of Oxygen."

"I'd have to check on that. But it doesn't matter. A month is too long to let a news show struggle. Besides, Traficant finally lost it."

Eric explained that Jim had gone too far with his guest, former Health and Human Services secretary and current University of Miami president Donna Shalala. Inexplicably he started screaming at her for pulling Miami out of the Big East and joining the

ACC, calling her first a secessionist, then a Nazi, a pinko, and finally a whore. Then he bit her. Shalala was fine; Traficant was in the hospital. Eric would be spinning this for weeks.

Before he could finish I realized that Eric would be making a number of calls as the MSNBC schedule began yet another reshuffle. This was perhaps my only opening.

"So what does this mean for me, Eric?" I said a little anxiously. "Do I finally get to go to the White House?"

"As a matter of fact," Eric began, "I do want you at the White House."

My heart began racing. "Oh, Eric, I'm just—"

He cut me off. "It's time the network had someone covering Barney."

"Barney who?"

"Barney Bush."

Silence.

"Barney is the President's dog," I said flatly.

"You're good," he laughed nervously. "I knew there was a reason we were in the Mo Rocca business. Sure you're not already covering this beat for us?" Eric had to know that this was something of a shock.

"Sorry if I seem thrown off, Eric. It's a lot to take in. I'm just trying to imagine my first question. Besides, doesn't Fox have someone on this beat?"

"Laurie Dhue is all over that story and it's been a real ratings winner for Fox News, so it's not going to be easy. But we believe there's room for a second voice. And, Mo, we know you have something to say."

"To a dog?"

"*About* a dog that happens to belong to the most powerful man in the world. You know, a lot of people believe that a pet is a window into a man's soul . . . or something like that."

"Something like that." I couldn't help but get snippy. "Oh, and forgive my snide question about talking to a dog. As we both know, Laurie Dhue is the only one in the press corps who gets any access to the First Dog."

"Yes, that is the challenge, Mo, one we expect you to meet." Eric's voice was sharpening. "Look, no one said this would be easy. Remember, you wanted to be in the White House, one of the toughest beats to snag. Now you're in the White House. You should be happy." Whether or not Eric believed what he said, I got the point. I needed to back off.

"Yes, of course," I said as humbly as possible. I had a lot of respect for Eric. He'd served his country valiantly in Gulf War I (also known as "Operation Let's See How It Goes And If It Doesn't Work Out We Can Always Come Back Later"). He had little patience for whining. "This should be exciting," I said with as much peppiness as I could muster. "Thank you, Eric."

Eric's voice brightened. "Good luck, Mo. And careful getting through that pressroom doggy door. It's a tight squeeze, I hear."

I hung up. Was I bitter? Not really, I was laughing. Okay, I was laughing bitterly. I'd never even had a dog and now I was going to be reporting full-time on one, against America's cable news sweetheart.

Laurie Dhue. Among the vast firmament of Fox News starlets Laurie was the brightest. Fox News chief Roger Ailes, the Louis B. Mayer of twenty-four-hour news, had early on chosen her as a favorite. She had the girl-next-door moxie of June Allyson and the lips of Lana Turner, shiny wet, like she had just eaten a pork chop. With the big blue eyes of Betty Hutton and the husky voice of Betty Bacall, she was the buxom blonde who appealed to all Fox News watchers, a wide-ranging group of conservative white men over fifty. Laurie was the Viagra in their Cialis.

It was a combination that had made her release of *Red, White and Barney: My First Dog* (Random House, $29.95) a gigantic best-seller last Christmas. The authorized "dogography" was a coffee-table book that featured a red-white-and-blue-clad Laurie frolicking with the Scottish terrier all over the South Lawn. The access she'd been granted was truly astonishing, though the book seemed to feature the author more than the subject. It's true that the "centerfold" shot of Laurie and Barney splashing in the fountain was split pretty evenly between reporter and dog, a "fair and balanced pose," the caption coyly read. I particularly liked the shot of a teary Laurie saluting our troops with one arm and snuggling Barney in the other at Andrews Air Force Base.

Some Democrats complained about the shot of the two of them in front of the FDR Memorial. Laurie sat in FDR's lap and Barney blocked the small statue of the thirty-second President's own Scottie, Fala. The Dems claimed that the shot was meant to suggest that Bush had eclipsed FDR as a "War President" but even they conceded that Laurie was a huge hit. "I about expected Roosevelt to get up from outta that chair, he must have been so excited," cracked Georgia senator and Fox News contributor Zell Miller.

Naturally Laurie became the envy of a whole bevy of Fox beauties. The vixenish newsreader Kiran Chetry called her "the Beltway Boys' Goodtime Girl," a reference to Fox's bad boys Morton Kondracke and Fred Barnes. The lusty Linda Vester whispered about "Laurie's Little Helpers," pills that she purportedly took to keep pace with her grueling studio schedule. These were all lies.

The luscious Laurie shrewdly held her head high and Mr. Ailes rewarded Laurie's hard work by giving her her own hour-long weekday show about the First Dog. *The Dig Story with Laurie Dhue* featured a "Daily Doggie Treat" (her version of O'Reilly's opening "Talking Points Memo"), fierce debates over pet care, clips from *Here's Boomer* and *Benji,* and a few car chases thrown in for good measure. On the screen, just above the terror alert, was a clock counting down to Barney's next birthday. Inset above that was a live shot of the entrance to Barney's doghouse. Alongside that was the temperature reading from inside the doghouse.

The show featured a parade of retired generals, former prosecutors, royal watchers, and administration representatives who came by, not only to gush over images of Barney, but also to remind Americans that Barney wanted us to support all the White House's initiatives.

As National Security Advisor Condoleezza Rice reasoned, "The President believes that true Americans love dogs, in particular Barney."

"And Barney, it is fair to say, loves the President," added Laurie.

"The President believes that that would be a logical extrapolation," Condi confirmed, before reaching a final computation. "Therefore it is the position of this administration that true Americans love the President." Case closed.

The network backed up Condi's contention with regular polls.

A weekly Fox News/Opinion Dynamics poll asked Americans if they liked Barney. An average of 94 percent said yes. A nearly equal number answered yes when asked if Barney liked the President.

In his lone appearance on *The Dig Story, Newsweek*'s Jonathan Alter questioned how America could be sure that Barney supported privatization of Medicare, a doctrine of preemption, and a constitutional amendment prohibiting same-sex marriage. He was promptly shouted down as a cat person by former Dukakis campaign manager and Fox News contributor Susan Estrich.

The political analysis sometimes took a darker turn. Former Clinton advisor Dick Morris occasionally dropped in to explain exactly how Hillary murdered Bill's Labrador Buddy in 2001.

But the emphasis of *The Dig Story* was upbeat and informative, and Laurie guided it all very skillfully. She'd brought the same enthusiasm and pearly white wattage to her earlier coverage of the standoff in Kashmir. Mr. Ailes and the rest of the News Corp. suits took notice. As for the locals, if Hindus and Muslims could agree on one thing, it was that Laurie's career was going nuclear. Their predictions were right on: within a year she was covering Barney and Fox News had increased its lead over CNN considerably. Fawning Internet bloggers instantly crowned her "Miss Shock and Paw."

The executives at CNN sniffed at their rivals' "craven disregard for hard news." "A full hour on a dog?" network president Jim Walton scoffed to a group of television critics not long after firing Connie Chung for the second time. CNN's coverage of Barney was only a half hour each day, he haughtily assured them, "unless of course a canine emergency warrants expanded coverage." Otherwise CNN would not give short shrift to the stories that mattered. "A little blond girl could very well be kidnapped in the next few weeks. Then once again people will discover that they can depend on CNN."

It was easy to get caught up in the insular world of cable news concerns. Yes, America did love Barney. He was an adorable dog. And apparently America couldn't get enough. But I couldn't help but wonder if that made him *newsworthy*. I needed to maintain perspective, so I called my father to get his reaction to my job offer. I suspected that he'd be disappointed, which might not be such a bad thing. I might then have the courage to hold out for something better.

"Wow, Laurie Dhue has very big lips," he murmured, before snapping out of his reverie. "Well, son, you made it to the White House. I'm proud."

"But, Pop, I'll be covering a dog."

"Who doesn't love dogs?" Then he sounded suspicious. "What are you, son? A cat person?"

"No," I answered defensively. "Of course not." My head was spinning and I needed a special kind of counsel. I hung up, then dialed a number I knew by heart and waited for the soothing voice on the other end. He picked up.

"Wolf, it's me," I said. "I need to see you."

5

The Karate Yid

As soon as I pulled into Wolf Blitzer's suburban Maryland driveway I began unwinding. Perhaps it was the balmy breeze blowing the chimes at the front entrance or the smell of jasmine in the air. I removed my shoes, placed them alongside two other pairs, took a deep breath, and rang the bell.

The door opened and immediately the smile warmed me. In his dragon-patterned kimono, Wolf was the personification of peace.

"Mo-san," he sighed, opening the screen door with one arm, embracing me with the other, then ushering me inside in one gentle fluid motion. I'd forgotten the sensation of tatami under my feet. "Forgive my informal appearance," Wolf said. He was wearing the cotton yukata kimono, rather than the more formal silk one. "I've just come from a very hot bath."

"Believe me, I'm just glad you could see me," I said.

"Well then, today is a day for the garden," Wolf intoned. "Mihoko," he said to his ancient serving girl, "could you bring us tea in the garden?" Mihoko set down her still-wet scrub brush and disappeared into the pantry. Wolf led me out through the back.

Wolf's Japanese tea garden was one of the Washington area's

best-kept secrets (as was the fact that Wolf is actually Japanese). A path of polished stepping-stones led down around a koi pond that held at least fifteen fish, some nearly a meter in length. Meiji-era stone lanterns flanked each end of a footbridge that led over the pond and into a small meditation house with shoji screen doors covered in a translucent, pine-laminated paper. A variety of evergreens, including a stunning collection of bonsais, warmed the environment. Outside the surrounding walls suburbia sprawled and honked. Inside Wolf's garden it was Kyoto before Commodore Perry's arrival. And Wolf was a master sensei.

We sat cross-legged by the koi pond.

"Bernie's gotten so big," I marveled, pointing at one of the fish, named after one of Wolf's former CNN colleagues.

"Fate has been kind," concurred Wolf.

Years before, I'd come to Wolf's garden seeking advice. My boss at CBS's *Early Show* had asked me to spend a week at Ringling Brothers Circus School learning to fly the trapeze, something Charlie Gibson from *Good Morning America* had done only three weeks before. After meditating, Wolf had advised me to call in sick rather than look like an also-ran. In exchange for his counsel I'd repainted the garden walls. It all seemed like yesterday.

"Now what troubles you this day?" Wolf asked now.

I explained my new assignment. "I'm torn, Wolf. I certainly don't want to run from my fate."

"Indeed. So much is preordained. It was my fate to have a beard. It was my fate to have this wonderful home and garden. It was my fate to spend months at a time in Qatar, a country pronounced far differently than it is spelled." He smiled. "It is okay to laugh."

I didn't realize he'd made a joke. I forced a chuckle.

"Remember, Mo-san," Wolf continued, "sometimes we must simply trust the plan that has been laid for us. Perhaps you are meant to report about a dog. The important thing is to pursue

LIVE

CNN **TSUNAMI APPROACHING**
WOLF BLITZER
DOW
105.35

WASABI PRICES SPIKE • "HELLO KITTY" TO LAUNCH NEW CHARAC

your destiny with mustard." He of course meant "relish." Wolf could be forgiven the occasional malaprop, having learned English in a California internment camp.

"So maybe I was meant to cover Barney? Because if I knew for sure that things would work out, I would give myself into fate and just—"

Wolf had risen to his feet, grabbed a bottle of Pledge, and moved over to a lovely lacquered console table against the wall, by the entrance to the house. He sprayed the table, then gently shushed me. "Wax on, wax off," he said as he wiped the table clean. As always I followed along and for a moment I felt genuinely transported to a happier plane, accompanied by a siren's song. (Mihoko was standing in the threshold singing.) When it was over the table looked great, and I felt as if I was walking on air. Whether or not it was the work of the lemon-fresh fumes didn't matter. The tension-related aches and pains of the last few hours disappeared.

Wolf led me to his crouching bowl (*tsukubai,* in Japanese) at the end of the garden to cleanse our hands and feet in the purifying waters. (I'd rigged the bamboo spout on yet another visit.) Mihoko followed, clack-clacking in her traditional geta sandals, and wrapped my feet in a hot towel before serving us tea.

"I feel better, Wolf."

"Clarity is good," he said, closing his eyes and tilting his peaceful Asiatic face up into the sun.

I knew what Wolf was trying to tell me. "This assignment could be a very good opportunity," I said. "I will cover Barney. Thanks, now I should go." I started to leave, but Wolf gently held me back and extended an open hand to me.

"When you can snatch these pebbles from my hand, it is time for you to leave."

Without thinking I snatched the pebbles.

"Great. Okay, now you really do have to leave. I'm subbing for Paula tonight and I'm interviewing Tito Jackson in about ninety minutes. It's an exclusive."

6

Fast Times at
White House High

The following Thursday was the first day of the rest of my life. I woke up at 4:30 in the morning, staring at the ceiling and rehearsing my first question for my first White House briefing. I hadn't felt such nervous excitement since the morning of my first day in the third grade after I'd left Catholic school and been thrown into the public school system. Would I make friends? Would I make good grades? Would I get knifed? (As a nine-year-old, I'd made the mistake of watching *Blackboard Jungle* the night before.)

I was as prepared as I could be, having acquired and read every book in the Presidential Pet canon. Niall Kelly's *Presidential Pets* was the best, superior to Vera Foster Rollo's *Presidents and Their Pets.* As for Janet Caulkins's *Pets of the Presidents,* it was too derivative. Margaret Truman—daughter of Harry—lent an insider's perspective to *White House Pets,* which was precisely its downside. She furiously spun her father's exiling of Mike, their Irish setter, to a Virginia farm. (She blamed Secret Service agents for feeding him candy and giving him rickets.)

As for Doris Kearns Goodwin's *No Ordinary Ferret,* it read suspiciously in parts like several of the others.

My studies had consumed me and I'd barely stepped outside in the last week, furiously taking notes on my research.

There were some interesting patterns, as many of the pets bore an uncanny resemblance to their owners. William Howard Taft, our fattest Chief Executive, had a Holstein cow named Pauline. Peace-lover Woodrow Wilson had a gentle sheep named Old Ike. (Old Ike delighted visitors with his habit of chewing tobacco. Just like Wilson's League of Nations, though, Old Ike suffered a sad end. He developed an addiction to nicotine and died a junkie on a Maryland farm.)

Andrew Jackson, the first "Common Man" president, kept a cursing parrot named Pol. Pol even screamed obscenities during Jackson's funeral service, doubtless to the delight of "Old Hickory's" risen spirit.

The misshapen Zachary Taylor (giant head, short legs) had an equally odd-looking horse, the knock-kneed Old Whitey. The Yankee Coolidges shared two very patrician collies, Prudence Prim and Rob Roy. And Teddy Roosevelt, the indomitable former asthmatic, adopted a one-legged rooster with almost manic energy. TR's children made a crutch for the bird. (With thirty-six pets, Teddy Roosevelt held the record for the most.)

Only Millard Fillmore didn't have a pet.

Then there were the exotic or just plain weird pets. The flamboyant Martin Van Buren had tiger cubs, a gift from the Sultan of Oman. (Sadly for Van Buren, Las Vegas's Mirage Hotel would not open for another 110 years.) The Marquis de Lafayette brought President John Quincy Adams an alligator, which the sixth President kept in the East Room, far from his and wife Louisa's collection of silkworms. Coolidge, in second place with thirty-three pets, also housed at various times a pygmy hippo, a wallaby, an antelope, a large white goose named Enoch, and a raccoon named Rebecca. And George Washington had a jackass named Royal Gift, a gift from the King of Spain and the progenitor of Mount Vernon's line of acclaimed "supermules," the best draft animals in Virginia.

Lincoln's dog Fido, the first presidential pet to be photographed. Animal lover Abe also had two goats named Nanny and Nanko, among other pets.

Benjamin Harrison's goat His Whiskers with Harrison's son Russell, three presidential grandchildren, and presidential dog Dash. The President himself had to chase down His Whiskers one day, after he raced off with the kids trailing in his cart.

Since World War II the pets were fewer and far less unusual. The best known was FDR's Scottie Fala, a gift from his cousin Margaret Suckley in 1940. Fala was not only beloved, he was a witness to history. He observed the Atlantic Charter summit aboard the USS *Augusta* alongside Churchill's poodle Rufus. Fala missed Yalta but he never missed a press conference. When Republicans charged that a naval destroyer had been sent, at great taxpayer expense, to retrieve Fala in the Aleutian Islands after being accidentally left behind in 1944, FDR shot back: "These Republicans have not been content with attacks on me, my wife, or my sons. No, not content with that, they now include

President Woodrow Wilson's sheep, including the tobacco-chewing ram Old Ike, kept the South Lawn shorn while the staff gardeners went off to battle during WWI.

my little dog, Fala." It was a strategy aped—er, copied—by Vice President Richard Nixon in his famous Checkers speech in 1952.

Of course I loved any excuse to indulge my passion for all things presidential. And there were moments during my week-long cram when I thought the subject of presidential pets might add up to something more than a collection of quirky factoids. But I quickly clipped my own wings. This assignment was simply an entryway to a more serious beat somewhere down the line, I hoped.

With First Pet trivia overcrowding my head, I walked down Connecticut Avenue, cut through Farragut Park, and turned onto 16th Street. The small but stately Hay-Adams Hotel stood on my right; St. John's, also known as "the church of the Presidents," on my left. And in front of me, across Lafayette Square, was the White House.

Since 1800 it stood there, burned by the British in 1814, gutted for renovation by Harry Truman in 1948, targeted by Al Qaeda in 2001. But the outer walls had never given way. (Truman had insisted that the original exterior remain intact during the reconstruction, for the important symbolic value. For his efforts he treated himself to a South Portico balcony, henceforth named the Truman Balcony.) Irishman James Hoban's neoclassical design for the Executive Mansion won out over the others—which, by the way, included Jefferson's—because it was dignified, not extravagant like that of a European monarch's palace.

Abigail Adams, the first First Lady to live there, had to hang her laundry in the East Room. And on the mantel down the hall in the State Dining Room a quotation of her husband's was still inscribed: "I Pray Heaven Bestow the Best of Blessings on This House and All that shall hereafter inhabit it. May none but Honest and Wise Men ever rule under this Roof."

I stopped for a moment, and, staring at the People's House, I felt a lump in my throat.

As I headed toward the northwest gate I thought of a deodorant ad from my childhood: Never let them see you sweat. I had to be confident, I told myself, as a few members of the press corps filed in ahead of me.

Easier said than done. The White House reporters wouldn't suffer fools gladly. They'd likely sneer at my beat—these were people covering America's political nerve center. But I had to believe I could win their respect. I knew a few of them socially, so that was some comfort. The ones who didn't know me would soon discover that I had a genuine interest in the inner workings of the presidency; that covering Barney was simply my way in, my dues paying.

I flashed my freshly laminated credential. The sergeant buzzed me in. I pushed open the wrought-iron gate, then made my way through the metal detector. Suddenly I was on the grounds. On my right was a phalanx of video cameras on tripods, where television correspondents did their live stand-up shots from a patch of ground known as Pebble Beach. (The area used to be covered in gravel.) It was a short walk up the driveway and past the fountain on my left. If I'd kept going straight I'd have run right into the sentry guarding the Oval Office, at the end of the West Wing. The distance was surprisingly short so I cut sharply left and entered through the French doors.

I was standing in the Briefing Room. The first of the day's two briefings, known as the gaggle, would not begin for at least ten minutes so I quietly disappeared into the pressroom next door.

This room, which contained the reporters' "offices," was underwhelming—just three short rows of cubicles, some more decorated than others, mostly unoccupied. The room was lined on three sides with booths for each of the broadcast networks and a few radio networks. I was struck first by the quiet, then by the smell, a combination of sweatsocks and stale French fries. The kitchen area stank. Downstairs, things were even dirtier.

I wasn't going to be given my own workspace, at least not anytime soon, so I timed my entrance so that I wouldn't have to stand awkwardly for too long. Upstairs I backed up against the beige-ish wall, hoping to blend in.

"Hey there, kiddo!" I turned to my left and down a bit to see a big smiling face.

"Andrea!" I hadn't seen NBC's pint-sized Andrea Mitchell in at least two years. "How are you?"

"How are *you*? I'm glad you survived Traficant."

"Just barely. Let's just say I'm happy for the furlough." She laughed, harder than she had to. She was a respected network reporter; I was from the bastard cable cousin. But she knew I needed the confidence boost. What I didn't need was the gratuitous brush of her hand against my backside. (I'd forgotten how everyone called her "Grabbyhands Mitchell" or "Handrea," for short.) I'd always wondered if her husband, Fed chairman Alan

Greenspan, had any idea how aggressive she could be. No matter, she was probably sweeter than anyone else in the press corps. In 1997 when I threw up at Jim Lehrer's Christmas party, she was the one who brought me upstairs and gave me a sponge bath.

"So you're covering the President," she said.

"Yes, that's right." I was, in a way.

"Good for you!" she cheered as she looked me up and down. "Nice to see you're working out," she added with a squeeze of my biceps. Before this could go any further a voice announced over the PA that the press briefing was beginning in two minutes.

I followed the crowd back into the James Brady Briefing Room, a space I'd seen countless times on television. It used to be the pool where FDR would swim for exercise. President Nixon had the floor boarded over and carpeted for briefings. The room certainly had a temporary feel. Six rows of eight high-school-auditorium-style seats were bolted into the uneven floor, which was covered in a stained carpet of indeterminate color (somewhere between gray and brown). The chairs faced the familiar press secretary's lectern, which was backed by a cheap blue curtain at the head of the room. A sign stuck on the drape read "The White House." The stucco ceiling hung low. Camera stands lined the sides and cluttered the back of the room. The walls were otherwise bare, except for one picture of Ronald and Nancy Reagan congratulating a wheelchair-bound former press secretary James Brady on the naming of the room. (At first glance I thought it was Larry Flynt.)

The room was so small, unimpressive, and uncomfortable. Nixon was smiling from his grave. This was his gift to the press corps.

As luck would have it, I did know some of the crowd that started trickling in, including Fox News's Jim Angle, who greeted me heartily.

"If you think it smells now, you should have been here yesterday. A dead muskrat was stuck behind one of the vending machines and, man, did it stink. I guess someone took care of it," he said. "So what do you think?"

As underwhelmed as I was by the surroundings, I couldn't help but think of the history that had taken place here. "To think that Roosevelt used to swim here does hit you kind of hard. Can you imagine the stress he was under?"

"Yeah, well maybe if he'd spent a little less time swimming and a little bit more time studying up on his 'Uncle Joe' Stalin, he wouldn't have given away Eastern Europe for the next forty-five years," he said.

Jim wasn't one of those conservatives still fighting the Cold War. He was busy battling the League of Nations. But he was also a nice guy and a big-time gambler. When I'd gone undercover as a blackjack dealer in Atlantic City I'd watched dumbstruck as he nearly cleaned out his buddy Bill Bennett. Afterward he'd taken me out drinking. I liked him.

"Glad to have my wingman on board. Just don't let the Clinton News Network people poison your mind," he said. "Oops, hope no one heard me," he added playfully.

"Put a sock in it, Angle," shot back CNN's Candy Crowley, Jim's sparring partner and one of the people I was looking forward to seeing most. "How's my boy?" Candy asked, slapping me on the back. I instantly felt much more at home.

Candy. She always played it sober and serious in interviews. In fact she had a biting, ribald wit and a heart of gold. She was an old-fashioned broad, the kind of woman Maureen Stapleton used to play, but saucier.

I'd met her at the 2000 Republican convention. I'd been sent by the *Early Show* to file a report on how delegates were keeping in shape. That's as close as they'd let me get to political coverage and I was very depressed. I met Candy at O'Flaherty's, an old Irish bar, and the hangout for Philly's political fixers. She was throwing back a sixth crème de menthe and she had the bartender in stitches, telling the story of how she'd run away from Bryn Mawr to follow a cowboy to Texas. It had been culture shock for a girl from a Main Line Philadelphia family who promptly disowned her, but she was in love. And yes, the ten-gallon hat she was wearing in the bar belonged to Chet.

Chet had died, though, she explained to everyone listening. Before long she had the whole joint in tears. Not Candy, though. "Why all the long faces?" she said.

That's when she noticed me. "You got a nice sensitive quality to you, kid. Kind of like Sal Mineo." We connected right away. Candy sympathized with my professional frustration. After a couple more drinks she pulled out her keys. "How about we go for a ride?"

An hour later Candy and I were flooring it through Amish country, the red top down on her Cadillac Eldorado, blaring Waylon Jennings. Candy loved outlaw country and Southern rock. I felt so alive with her.

She was an inspiration when I needed it—a true individual who'd risen through the ranks of a profession that often rewarded conformity. Eyebrows were raised when she took up with Pasquale, a young dishwasher she'd met at D.C.'s Florida Avenue Grill, but she didn't care. "He's the one," she said, even though she knew damn well that this wouldn't be the last in her long line of December-May romances—and that's the way she liked it.

When I found out that Candy packed heat—a pearl-handled revolver she'd been given by Chet's mother—I wasn't surprised. Interestingly she also had one of the Washington area's biggest collection of Hummel porcelain figurines. "I like delicate pretty things." Indeed Candy had the most beautifully manicured hands I'd ever seen.

She'd tried to quit her two-pack-a-day Benson & Hedges habit—alternating between the patch and Nicorette—but any weakness she still had only made you like her more. She was the

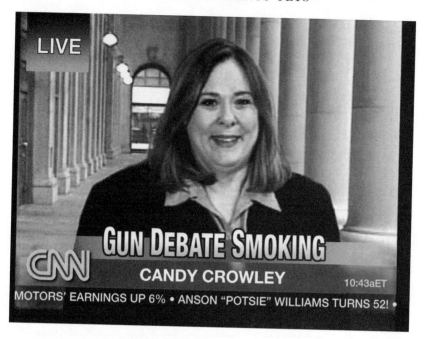

anti–John King. (King was CNN's other White House reporter, an ultra-fastidious squeaky-clean control freak. "That man's favorite book is *The South Beach Diet*," Candy once said.)

I hadn't seen Candy in ages, so I was thrilled when she sat down next to me in the middle of the room. "Good to see you're alive, pal. Traficant as big a bruiser as I've heard?"

Candy was off and running. As happy as I was to see her, I knew I'd get tired fast of her prison-rape jokes. "No, Candy," I sighed, "Traficant never laid a hand on me. But I can't say I'm sorry that the show's over."

"Is that what he called it? A 'show'? When I interviewed Rostenkowski in the pen he called it 'initiation.' Off the rec, of course. So," Candy continued, "you're finally covering *el Presidente*."

"Uh, yeah."

"What's 'uh, yeah'? Already phoning it in on your first day, amigo?"

"Well, Candy," and I lowered my voice, "I'm actually covering Barney. The dog."

Candy turned serious. "Oh, boy, you're gonna have a time of it getting access. Dhue's up that dog's ass like nobody's business. You know, tonight's the big party for her book. Fifty-two weeks on the best-seller list. Everyone is caught up in the hype." I found that hard to believe. The public might be Barney-crazy but official Washington, and surely the press corps, weren't going to be swept up so easily.

And yet as I looked around, the briefing room looked less like the newsroom in *All the President's Men* and more like the scene in my high school cafeteria.

A hierarchy was brutally apparent. "Those are the popular kids," said Candy, pointing to the first two rows, where reporters from the broadcast networks and the major dailies sat. NBC's cool redheaded Norah O'Donnell gossiped with the *Washington Post*'s wickedly funny Dana Milbank. ABC's blond and perky Kate Snow flirted with the tall, dark, and handsome correspondent from Agence France-Presse.

Meanwhile varsity TV reporting studs David Gregory and Terry Moran jock-talked about the previous day's Redskins game.

"If they like you enough, they might even invite you to join their spring-break house in Cancun," Candy said about the clique.

The third and fourth rows weren't so bad—the *New York Daily News* and NPR were here—but the last two rows were glum. "Loser city," said Candy, pointing to reporters from the *Akron Beacon Journal* and the *Milwaukee Sentinel,* both of them slumped in their chairs eating crumb cake. The reporter from the *St. Louis Post-Dispatch* passed gas audibly. "Real nice," said Terry Moran. The guy from the *Sacramento Bee* just scratched himself, then fell back asleep.

John King trailed in seconds later. He'd been finishing his morning crunches in an empty cubicle down the hall.

"So I guess everyone will turn it loose when Scott McClellan gets here," I said to Candy, pointing to the door that the press secretary used to enter the room.

Candy laughed. "You are adorable, kid. Sorry to say, not a lot gets turned loose around here, except the old girl over there," she said, turning her head toward Helen Thomas. "Poor thing."

While we were looking toward the back of the room, legendary White House reporter Helen Thomas had taken a free seat on the side and was furiously taking notes. A living breathing institution sat a few feet from me.

I didn't know any more about Helen Thomas than you could learn from any kid on any street corner in America—that since joining the White House press corps in 1961, the five-foot-three raven-haired Detroit-raised daughter of Lebanese immigrants had covered an unprecedented nine presidents, grilling them with hawklike determination and earning the moniker "Dean of the White House Press Corps." After her boss at UPI, Merriman Smith, died on April 13, 1970, she became the first female chief correspondent covering the White House, then the first female president of the White House Correspondents Association. Notoriously dogged, she was the only print reporter who accompanied Nixon to China.

Since then she'd never shirked her responsibility to ask uncomfortable questions. Ford called her methods a "fine blend of journalism and acupuncture." Clinton called her "the embodiment of fearless integrity." And every presidential press conference ended with her saying, "Thank you, Mr. President." Every press conference, that is, until March 6, 2003, when President Bush not only refused to call on her to ask a question, but also ended the press conference himself.

But that's really all I knew about her.

Helen Thomas, Dean of the White House Press Corps.

For some time Helen had been portrayed as something of a crazy old lady, the Norma Desmond of the White House press corps. Mind you, she was still the same notorious hard worker, who trudged into work at 6:30 A.M. most days. Yes, she'd left UPI in 2000, but she was now writing a syndicated column for Hearst.

I'd never met Helen Thomas but I'd always wondered: Did the press secretary's increasingly mocking responses to her questions bother her? At most she seemed bemused by his sarcasm. Many reporters I'd met cruelly mocked her behind her back. They said they teased her because they loved her. I could only imagine how the "popular" reporters treated her. Our eyes met for a moment and I turned away.

As everyone took their seats a fresh-faced Laurie Dhue rushed in, escorted by CBS's John Roberts, the John Davidson–handsome heir apparent to Dan Rather. They looked like a star quarterback and head cheerleader. A buzz went through the room as John whispered something in Laurie's ear and she tossed her head back with a laugh. Norah O'Donnell shot them a jealous look from behind her makeup compact. It was hard not to be envious: Laurie looked amazing. In her red gingham dress she was more radiant than Kim Novak in *Picnic*.

Finally the door behind the lectern opened and press secretary Scott McClellan walked in followed by four press aides. Three of the aides were absolutely unremarkable-looking. The fourth was hard to miss.

"Candy, who is that?" I asked.

"His name is Ernst Gephardtzenhopf," said Candy. "We call him Gephardt. Gephardt the Albino."

It wasn't just Gephardt the Albino's milk-white skin and hair or his pink eyes that struck me. He was tall and hulking, looming over the three other aides. His mien was profoundly serious, no, make that angry. He was, in a word, terrifying. He gave the room a once-over, pausing ever so slightly when he came to me. After registering my presence he settled into his seat.

I couldn't help but notice an unnatural bunching around his right upper arm, just below the shoulder. What did he have tied up there? I wondered.

Scott walked up to the podium and began listlessly reading his statement: "The President is currently reviewing troop movements in Sri Lanka and renewed tensions in the Golan Heights. The President and First Lady regret the passing of R&B legend Shirley Horn. The President will continue to press for a reduction in capital gains for our nation's seniors." No one bothered to write anything down. "Any questions?"

A gasp came from the back corner. Everyone turned and saw a red-faced Joe Klein (*Time* magazine) pulling away from Andrea Mitchell's grasp. Scott raised an eyebrow: "The President would like to advise the chairman of the Fed to spend less time watching the markets and more time watching his wife." Everyone laughed.

"Jesus, she's horny," said Candy, loudly enough for everyone to hear. "Looks like the only thing goin' up with Greenspan these days is interest rates." Candy raised her hand behind her, and Jim Angle, on cue, gave her five up top. This was a tough crowd.

After a few halfhearted questions about the President's forthcoming appearance on *The Tonight Show*—"Is the President afraid of getting 'Jay-walked'?"—Helen raised her hand. With the biggest sneer he could muster, Scott called on her: "Yes, *Helen?*"

"Why has the President refused to demand an explanation for Pakistani president Pervez Musharraf's acquiescence to continued incursions by Pakistani militants into Indian-controlled Kashmir?"

"Loser," coughed NPR's Nina Totenberg under her breath. Kate Snow cackled when David Gregory mimicked Helen from behind her.

Dana Milbank couldn't resist: "Excuse me, ma'am, can I get your autograph? My grandmother *loved* you on *Murder, She Wrote.*"

Scott took a deep breath: "Well, *Helen,*" he began as if he were speaking to a learning-disabled child, "the President doesn't condone such attacks. But, *Helen,* the President enjoys a close relationship with President Musharraf. So, *Helen,* the American people can rest assured that the American President will be very honest, *Helen,* with the Pakistani leader if warranted. Okay, *Helen?*"

Helen, unafraid, looked Scott right in the eye. "That's not okay, Scott. I need you to answer my question." But Helen's efforts to press her question were met by hisses from her fellow reporters.

"Hello-o? Please shut u-up," said Norah O'Donnell. A few reporters seconded her. Others laughed. Bill Moyers flung a Cheeto at her.

Even the *New York Times*'s germ warfare expert Judith Miller joined in: "Looks like we found our WMD—Woman of Massive Dementia!"

Helen pressed on. "If the American people are going to commit their sons and daughters to fighting terrorism, but a so-called partner in the fight continues—"

"This is really getting old, Helen. Your insubordination has been well noted by this White House." Scott scowled, then looked around for the next questioner. His face suddenly lit up. "Yes, Laurie!"

Like an A student getting ready to deliver an A+ report, Laurie flipped her hair back, cleared her throat, and referred to her notes. "Mr. Secretary, the public has been made aware that yesterday Barney had tummy problems. Mr. Secretary, America wants to know: did he do a nice poopie today?"

It was hard to believe that that question had just been asked in the White House Briefing Room. It seemed a violation of decorum and I was deeply embarrassed for Laurie. But rather than snickers and jeers, the only sounds were deeply concerned oohs and aahs.

Scott became very solemn. "Laurie, the First Family appreciates America's warm thoughts and prayers for Barney. Yesterday the First Dog indeed felt terrible. After an initial consultation, the White House vet wasn't sure what would happen. Barney was subsequently sent to Walter Reed Medical Center. As of this morning Barney's prognosis was unclear . . ."

Kate Snow gasped, both hands to her mouth. The suspense was too much for her. Gil, the reporter from Agence France-Presse, wasn't sure what was happening but he put his arm around Kate to comfort her. A tear came to the eye of the *NASCAR Dads Daily* correspondent. (He had a permanent seat in the Briefing Room.) The news must have been killing Laurie, but she kept her cool.

Scott continued. "I can now announce that Barney is, after a brief scare"—and a big grin came over his face—"back to normal."

The pressroom broke into applause. Kate threw her arms around Gil, who bellowed *"Vive le chien!"* Everyone laughed, overjoyed. Laurie, a consummate pro, kept back the tears but couldn't hold back her thousand-watt smile.

"Thank you, Mr. Secretary. Thank you very much."

"My pleasure, Laurie. Thank *you* for restoring dignity to today's gaggle. As for everyone else, please remember that everything I said today, have said in the past, or will say in the future is, of course, off the record. Now if there are no further questions, let's adjourn this—"

"No, I have a question." Everyone had begun packing up, so I had to speak up loudly enough to be heard over the din. I was surprised that a poop should warrant so much attention from America's top reporters, but right now I had to focus on making a good first impression. I needed to ask something, if only to register my presence. Scott gave me an impatient look. I froze.

Candy nudged me. "Come on, big boy. Time to get it up."

I swallowed hard and dove right in. "Well," I began. "It seems to me, I mean, it seems to many that the President's strategy—or should I say, several leading historians—that's right, several historians have recently suggested that the President's initial congressionalist approach to economic policy, strikingly similar to President McKinley's, has been largely re-formed due to the lingering economic troubles, so that what we see now is something much more activist, even Rooseveltian—fitting perhaps"—and here's where I tied it all together—"when you consider that both this President and FDR had Scotties."

The silence was almost soothing, meditative. If it had gone on forever it might have seemed like the nirvana Buddhists pray for, an emancipation from worldly evils, a final absorption into the divine. But it was a state of nothing, a vacuum that needed to be filled. And ridicule and contempt poured in from every corner. First Scott's laugh, then Terry Moran's, then John Roberts's. Kate Snow just pointed at me, laughing so hard her knees buckled.

Scott wiped the tears from his eyes, that's how hard he was laughing. "I'm sorry, but aren't you the guy who wears the mustache on . . . MSNBC?!"

"It's Traficant's bitch!" yelled the *NewsHour*'s Elizabeth Farnsworth.

Candy put her arm around me. "You poor knucklehead."

Scott calmed everyone down and managed to stop smiling. "To answer your question, *Maurice,*" he chuckled, "let me say, for the record, that the President had no intention of ever adopting McKinley's economic model." And then the demonic grin crept back. "He's always been more of a John Tyler type of guy!"

The pressroom was roaring now.

"But that's not possible," shouted David Gregory, always the comedian. "Unless Tyler had a Scottie, too, right?"

"Tyler had two canaries and an Italian greyhound," I calmly responded, unintentionally setting off another explosion of derisive laughter. The only one not laughing was Gephardt the Albino. He just fixed me with a cold stare.

"Have a great weekend, everyone," said a laughed-out McClellan. And he was out the door followed by his aides. Everyone got up and still giggling regrouped into their respective cliques and started out the front entrance. A large group followed after Laurie, copying off her notes.

"You hang in there, tiger," said Candy as she gathered her things and put a cigarette in her mouth. "But take it from me: Stick with the crap line of questions." She snapped her fingers toward Angle. "Hey, rightie, got a lightie?" Angle lit her up and they exited. I began to pack my things in my backpack and made a mental note to get a briefcase.

"I liked your question," came a voice from behind. I quickly turned, assuming it was Andrea Mitchell.

"Thanks, Andrea," I said. "Oh, I'm sorry, Ms. Thomas. I thought you were—"

"You don't need to be so formal. It's Helen." Standing next to me Helen Thomas was nearly a foot shorter than I. "Want some trail mix?" She held out a bag of what looked like dried leaves and grass.

"No, thank you."

"So I like the way you approached your question. It sounds like you know your stuff. You know, the only reason they gave you a hard time is because you had the guts to ask a tough question. A lot of them lost heart long ago."

"I don't know. I'm afraid it was a bit of a convoluted question."

"Made sense to me. And don't worry, the White House can handle smart questions, even if they try to make you think otherwise."

"Well, thank you for being so supportive," I said. "Coming from you, I mean, you were a big reporter."

"I *am* a big reporter," she snapped. "It's just the typeset that got smaller."

"Forgive me, Helen," I blurted. "I meant to say that you're an institution. Not that you're old or anything!" I kept fumbling with my words, I was so nervous.

She smiled. "I'm just kidding, dear. Of course I'm old," she laughed. It was a strange warbling laugh. "But let me tell you, some things never change around here. Believe it or not, James Garfield's press aide was even meaner, so don't feel sorry for me or yourself."

I appreciated her reassurance, although it seemed an odd example. If Helen were talking about a press secretary she actually knew—for instance, JFK's Pierre Salinger—I'd have been truly impressed.

"I probably should take more time to read about our nation's press secretaries," I said, not quite sure how to respond. Still I immediately had a good feeling about this woman. She could have blown me off and yet she seemed much more human than anyone else here, despite her unusual appearance.

She was a short squat woman with a small, almost beaklike mouth covered in lipstick. Where the lipstick had smudged I could see that her lips were a pale yellowish white color. Helen's eyes, her best feature, were closely set and dark brown, almost black. Attractive and modest, from certain angles she looked like a cross between Nancy Walker and Anna Magnani. From pictures I'd seen, she rarely wore anything that revealed more than her face and neck. Up close her skin was redder than it appeared on TV and her brunette hair stiff. The roots appeared to be red.

More important than her looks, Helen Thomas was a witness to so much history. If she was willing to talk to me, I wasn't going to waste the opportunity. "I'd love to pick your brain, hear some stories sometime, about all you've seen," I said. "No one knows more about the presidency than you do."

"Oh, I love to share what I know," she said before leaning in and lowering her voice. "The most important thing is *to dig deeper.*" She was awfully close, but I didn't want to be rude.

"Well, that sounds like great advice. Listen, I packed a couple of sandwiches—trying to save money—so maybe we could go across the street to Lafayette Park and talk some more."

"No, thanks," she said. "Pastrami and sauerkraut on rye with Russian dressing isn't for me."

"Wow, how did you know that's what I packed?"

Helen became skittish. "Well, you told me—a few minutes ago. Don't you remember? Of course you do. Besides, I already ate."

"Well then maybe we can just get a drink or—"

Then Helen began gagging.

"Are you okay?"

She looked terribly embarrassed but couldn't stop herself. I was about to call someone for help when Helen finally coughed up a small pellet. It flew past me and landed on the floor.

I turned around, then reached down to look at it. The pellet consisted of dried hair and bone material. I immediately recognized one of the tiny bone shards as that of a young muskrat tibia.

"Helen, are you sure you don't need to see a—?" But when I turned back around, Helen had vanished, flown the coop in a flash.

7

Vanity Fair and Balanced

Candy was right. That night everyone who was anyone turned out to fete Laurie's fifty-two weeks on the *Times* best-seller list. Washington's ritzy Anderson House, home to the Society of the Cincinnati, was packed to the gills with stars of every stripe—from front-page politicians to Page Six celebs—and the sidewalk was crammed with camera-toting gawkers. Fox News was covering the event exclusively, though Eric had ordered me to try to get a piece of the action. But when Phil the cameraman and I showed up, we were told that we would not be welcome past the velvet rope. We would have to shoot from across the street.

Fox's Jimmy Olsen–like Carl Cameron was just outside the mansion wrapping up an interview with Senate majority leader Bill Frist and *The Simple Life*'s Nicole Richie, who'd just finished addressing a Senate panel on the need for increased ethanol subsidies, so I waited patiently before pleading my case. "Come on, Carl, can't I bring the crew inside just for a second?"

"Sorry, Mo. Mr. Ailes is in there," he said, "and he just wouldn't allow it." Carl lowered his voice. "Look, why don't you just shoot me interviewing some of the arrivals? I'll pretend I don't see you doing it."

Covering Fox News's coverage of its own event didn't feel journalistically right, but as everyone in cable understood, there was only so much breaking news to go around. On the bright side, maybe one day someone from CNBC would cover my coverage of Fox News's coverage of . . . you get the idea.

Of course before we could do anything I needed to get Phil's attention, but he was back on the phone: "So, Norma, just guess where the President is campaigning tomorrow. Okay, I'll tell you. *Carlisle,* Pennsylvania. Coincidence? I think not."

Naturally I wanted to get this done as quickly as possible so that I could get rid of Phil.

Once we got our shot, I decided to stick around. I wanted to see inside this Washington power shindig for myself. With a nod from Carl to the doorman, I was waved through.

It was Hollywood on the Potomac. An imposing Roger Ailes sat in a giant thronelike armchair chomping on a cigar. A newly platinum blond Greta Van Susteren, looking more like Jean Harlow than ever before, sat on one arm; Barbara Stanwyck look-alike Mara Liasson foxed it up on the other.

The mixture of power and glamour created a cocktail so heady that artificial barriers—like network affiliation or party membership—evaporated. Bill O'Reilly, author of *Stickin' Up for You: Lessons from a Working Class Non-Partisan Populist from Levittown* (#3 on the best-seller list) shared a drink with Senator Hillary Clinton, whose sequel memoir *Living More History* was stuck at #4 on the list. Both knew they didn't stand a chance of knocking Laurie off the top spot.

Nor did Bill Clinton (#2 on the list), who seemed especially upbeat. Grinning ear to ear this night, the forty-second President was wearing sunglasses and "double-fisting"—teen queen Hilary Duff under one arm and her archrival Lindsay Lohan under the other. "C'mon, girls," whooped Clinton hoarsely, "if I could bring Arafat and Rabin together . . ."

ALL THE PRESIDENTS' PETS

Everyone laughed, including conservative writer Bernie Goldberg. His latest effort, *Diatribe,* was stuck at #5, despite a blockbuster quote attributed to his nemesis, the liberal columnist Paul Krugman: "Americans[1] . . . should[2] . . . stab[3] . . . President Bush[4] . . . in[5] . . . the[6] . . . head.[7]"

Creating quite a stir were former NOW president Patricia Ireland and Fox News *Special Report* anchor Brit Hume, the two of whom were dancing a mean lambada. The two had bonded the year before, at a callback audition for HBO's canceled series *K Street.*

Surely these people had very real differences with each other. But they all seemed to understand that like supporting a White House at war, supporting the First Pet was a political must. And at a gathering like this, there was much to be gained. Former *Dharma & Greg* star Jenna Elfman might find a back-of-the-book quotation for her Scientology-themed celebrity children's book, *Sarah Clear and Tall.* Senator Orrin Hatch might convince Snoop Dogg to sing a track on his next album of patriotic songs.

Tart-tongued and ubiquitous defense attorney Gloria Allred was there, accompanied by wheelchair-bound physicist Stephen Hawking. Gloria had recently achieved the elusive Cable News

---

1. From "Going for Broke" by Paul Krugman, *The New York Times,* January 20, 2004, Tuesday, Late Edition—Final, Section A, Page 19, Column 6, Editorial Desk.
2. From "The Awful Truth" by Paul Krugman, *The New York Times,* January 13, 2004, Tuesday, Late Edition—Final, Section A, Page 25, Column 6, Editorial Desk.
3. From "The Real Thing" by Paul Krugman, *The New York Times,* August 20, 2002, Tuesday, Late Edition—Final, Section A, Page 19, Column 6, Editorial Desk.
4. From "The China Syndrome" by Paul Krugman, *The New York Times,* September 5, 2003, Friday, Late Edition—Final, Section A, Page 19, Column 1, Editorial Desk.
5. From "Who Gets It?" by Paul Krugman, *The New York Times,* January 16, 2004, Friday, Late Edition—Final, Section A, Page 21, Column 1, Editorial Desk.
6. From "Enron and the System" by Paul Krugman, *The New York Times,* January 9, 2004, Friday, Late Edition—Final, Section A, Page 19, Column 1, Editorial Desk.
7. From "Waggy Dog Stories" by Paul Krugman, *The New York Times,* May 30, 2003, Friday, Late Edition—Final, Section A, Page 27, Column 1, Editorial Desk.

Trifecta: in defiance of the time-space continuum she had managed to appear live in studio on all three cable news channels simultaneously. Hawking was convinced she held the secret to understanding the wormhole.

Through his computerized voicebox Hawking enthused, "Laurie Dhue beautiful. Party great."

This *was* a great party, which was why the drab print media, generally so aloof when it came to television news events, couldn't stay away. The *New York Times*'s reporter Linda Greenhouse came in Ugg boots and nearly fainted when *Access Hollywood* host Pat O'Brien told her what a fan he was of her Supreme Court coverage. (Yes, Ugg boots were so last year, but the *Times* was still playing catch-up on its style coverage.) Conservative mandarin and wordsmith William Safire was only too happy to explain to Tyra Banks that a Pekingese is not necessarily from the city currently named Beijing.

Gliding through the room, decked out in vintage Givenchy and looking like Grace Kelly, Laurie beamed, graciously accepting a compliment from Queen Noor here, a "You go!" from Queen Latifah there. Henry Kissinger and Christopher Hitchens, friends after Laurie had brought them together, toasted her. "Laurie, I'm so happy for you I just feel like giggling!" tittered Hitchens.

A momentary hush came over the crowd when Walter Cronkite rose and pronounced Laurie a credit to the profession and congratulated her on being named *Entertainment Weekly*'s Presidential Dog "It Girl."

Through it all a doddering Liz Smith sat in the corner scribbling down celebrity names for her next column. "Does anyone know how to spell Lainie Kazan?" she muttered to no one in particular.

Things were a little raunchier in back where pudgy FCC overlord Michael Powell was receiving a lap dance from Courtney Love. It was hard not to be distracted by the jiggling of his own man breasts. (At least he was wearing pasties.) Conservative pit-bull Sean Hannity looked on intensely as liberal Alan Colmes fidgeted nervously.

I downed one tumbler of Scotch as fast as I could, then another. Before I got too buzzed I realized my stomach was empty so I made my way over to the buffet table. I hadn't been eating well lately so I fixed myself a salad.

Beside the buffet table sat a spruced-up kennel with five dogs in it, the only nod to the purported subject of Laurie's book. They were each dressed up as different Presidents. They looked sad. No doubt Laurie and many of the guests here were pet owners. But these defenseless creatures were being ignored, relegated to props in Fox News's transparent bid to show how all-American they were.

A beagle dressed as Washington was particularly compelling. He fixed his eyes on me and I couldn't resist moving closer.

"Hey there, boy, how ya doin'?" I said.

"A Salad Mincer," he said.

The dog talked. It wasn't the Scotch talking. I'd only been drinking for about twenty minutes.

"What?" I said stupidly.

"Oh, you guys are BAAAAAAAD!" I turned to see ultra–right wing and ex–MSNBC talk show host Michael Savage, a dangerously teetering Cosmo in hand, being propped up by the rest of Bravo's *Queer Eye for the Straight Guy* cast. Michael was the brand-new Fashion Guy, a promotions stunt that had added some oomph to the show's flagging ratings. (The original Fashion Guy, Carson Kressley, was booted off the show after his wife and two kids stepped forward and demanded that he stop living a lie and return to his native West Virginia.) The New Fab Five were coming toward me.

I turned back to the beagle. He was sniffing the dachshund's ass now. "What did you say?" I asked again.

"I said, 'You guys are B-A-D, BAAAAAAAAD!' " Michael leaned up against the kennel. "Hiya, sailor, have you met Ted, Jai, Thom, and . . ."

"Kyan," said the Hair Guy, clearly losing his patience.

"All of youse, don't be so baaaaad," slurred Michael. "So what's your name?"

The last thing I wanted to do was get acquainted with Michael Savage. A beagle had just spoken to me.

Before I could shake him, though, the kennel was being wheeled out by two workmen. "Where are the dogs going?" I asked a young woman who seemed to be in charge.

"Back to the agency. They're rentals," she said. Just as the kennel was disappearing through the double doors leading out to the loading dock, though, the beagle slipped out and darted ahead. No one else seemed to notice.

"Wait!" I shouted and ran out through the doors.

Out on the loading docks, the young woman was taking notes on the animals. "Okay, you're good to go," she said to the workmen.

"No, you're not. You just lost a dog," I huffed.

She looked at me blankly. "We came with four. We're leaving with four."

"But the beagle. You're leaving him behind. You can't just—"

"Sir, there was no beagle," she said.

"But I know I saw—"

"You heard the lady," said a vaguely Germanic monotone voice. "There was no beagle." I turned to see Gephardt the Albino staring down at me. My blood was chilled.

8

The Lair Down There

All night long I thought about what the beagle had said to me. "A Salad Mincer." Was this some sort of anagram? Anagrams were a passion of mine so I instantly decoded the beagle's message as an anagram for, among other things, "A Carnal Deism" and "A Manacled Sir." But they didn't seem to mean anything.

The next day's White House press briefing was relatively quick. My question was also much more concise: "Mr. Secretary, Andrew Johnson left scraps of cheese for the mice that lived in the White House during his term." True indeed. "Is the President concerned that Wisconsin's economic troubles may put that swing state firmly in the Democrats' column?" I must say it was a crafty way of asking a current-events question in the guise of my beat, and this time no one laughed. Granted, most everyone was hungover, including Scott, who had shown up at the party after I had left.

"No I don't think so . . . well, maybe . . . Whatever . . . it's all off the record," Scott trailed off. "See you tomorrow."

Candy got up to leave. "Hey, kiddo, join me at the Outback tonight at 8 P.M. A few of us are getting together to throw back a couple. If you haven't been there before, the Bloomin' Onion is delish." John King passed by, holding his gym bag. Candy couldn't resist taking a shot. "Hey, Johnny boy, need a lift to soccer practice?"

"Very funny, Candy," said John pertly. "FYI, I'm going to a spinning class and I'm driving myself, thank you." And he was off.

"So will I see you later?" Candy asked me.

"Sure, I'll be there." I was only half listening. I wanted to catch up with Helen before she left the building.

I caught her just as she was walking into the pressroom. "Hello, Helen. Have you got a second?"

"Of course, Mo dear. I'm sorry our conversation ended so abruptly yesterday. I was awfully rude, I'm afraid. I hope you're not upset with me." She seemed genuinely embarrassed.

"Oh please, Helen, that's absurd. I was afraid that you might not be well and I was just rambling on. Believe me, I have no bone to pick with you." That last sentence seemed to make her wince. "I just wanted to take you up on your offer, to hear some old stories, get some advice. I think I'm going to need it."

She smiled. "You're going to be fine, Mo. You've got to have tenacity in this business, especially with this White House. Something tells me you're pretty dogged." That last word startled me, considering the previous night's canine occurrence. Of course I didn't want to let my imagination wander in Helen's presence.

"So what do you say?" I offered. "Can we maybe grab a cup of coffee? There's a Starbucks at Farragut North."

She cut me off. "Follow me." Then in a hushed tone, "I know where we can find some peace and quiet."

"Careful, she likes 'em young," snickered Dana Milbank as we left together, not onto the North Lawn, but down the stairs to the lower floor of the pressroom. I wasn't sure where Helen was taking me.

"Nut job," coughed Nina Totenberg as we passed her on the stairs.

Helen took me to her tiny cubicle way in the back corner. It was fairly cluttered with books, papers, and issues of *Reader's Digest* dating back to 1911. The floor needed a good vacuuming, seeing as it was covered in a danderlike fuzz. A pair of sensible shoes sat by the wall.

"Are those Easy Spirit shoes?" I asked. "My great-aunt used to wear—Ouch!"

Without warning Helen had grabbed my wrist with her hand—it felt more like a claw—and yanked me under the desk. With lightning speed she pushed through the lower part of the wall. Suddenly we were crouched in some sort of crawl space.

The White House, like any old mansion, has all sorts of tiny nooks and crannies, maybe even secret rooms. Was this the room where Clinton had allegedly menaced Kathleen Willey? According to her testimony, she had a can of Diet Coke as a last line of defense. I only had my notepad and a copy of *Cat Fancy* magazine, which coincidentally had a great article on former First Cat Socks.

"Helen, what's going on?"

Helen wasn't wasting any time. She made sure the hatch behind us was closed tight, then dragged me down a passageway, through another door and down a long dusky stairwell. It all happened so quickly that I was convinced nobody saw us. But where were we? I knew there was at least one basement level; it was on all the available floor plans of the White House. It was my understanding that with the gutting of the White House during the Truman administration at the beginning of the Cold War, that another lower level was added—a bunker for the President and his staff for The Day After and beyond. But we seemed to be going lower than any imaginable bunker. Was this the secure location where Dick Cheney lived during orange alerts?

Just as it turned pitch black, the stairs ended and we came up against a wall. Helen went rummaging through her big black purse, pulled out an ancient and oversize key, then unlocked a thick steel door. She pushed it forward and we stepped inside.

Suddenly we were standing in a Victorian parlor, or secret annex. Gaslight fixtures illuminated tattered dark red silk damask wallpaper. The floors were covered with contrasting and overlapping oriental carpets, all of which clashed with the walls, as was the fashion in the mid-nineteenth century.

In the middle of the room was a large round pedestal table onto which Helen tossed her purse. In the center of the table sat a majestic marble bust that looked eerily like Helen. It must have been a coincidence, though, since I recognized the initials at its base as those of late-eighteenth-century French sculptor Jean-Antoine Houdon. "You like the bust?" asked Helen. "Tony was the best."

A small rosewood piano—similar to one I'd seen at the Ulysses S. Grant home in Galena, Illinois—sat close by. "It's actually a melodian," Helen said. "And it's a heck of a lot easier to play than the harpsichord."

On the far wall several ceiling-high shelves of books lined up perpendicularly to the rest of the room. It wasn't clear how far back they went.

Helen kicked off her shoes, plopped herself down on a Turkish daybed—not unlike one I'd seen at James Garfield's house in Mentor, Ohio—and propped herself up against a red velvet pillow. "Take a load off," she said.

I was speechless. Rather than sit down on her horsehair ottoman—a dead ringer for the one at James Buchanan's Wheatland estate in Lancaster, Pennsylvania—I wanted to explore every inch of Helen's lair. No one would ever believe me when I'd tell them what I'd seen, but at least I could remember it for myself.

The most intriguing piece was a massive mahogany cabinet against the wall opposite where Helen now reclined. On display on one shelf were mementos and curios from Helen's career at the White House, chief among them autographed pictures of her with different Chief Executives dating back to Kennedy. But I was more interested in the shelf above, which was lined with pictures of all the different presidential pets. Digital, Polaroids, black-and-whites, daguerreotypes, even a miniature Gilbert Stuart portrait of what appeared to be Washington's beloved steed Nelson.

"What a lovely lithograph," I said, pointing to another piece. "I've never seen a representation of John Quincy Adams's silkworms."

"I like that, too. Getting Henry Adams to part with it was a bitch." Peculiar. Henry Adams, grandson of John Quincy, died in 1918.

"There's so much I want to ask right now, Helen. For starters, where am I?"

"This is my home. It's been here for . . . a long time." Helen paused, and she sat deep in thought for a moment. "I only want to tell you what I think you can handle, Mo. I'd rather we move slowly. It's better for the both of us."

I was a bit indignant that I'd been dragged halfway to the center of the earth below the White House only to be told that I'd have to wait for the explanation. But I was also thrilled. Helen had literally opened a door to a place I didn't know existed. For the first time in my career I could very well be on to something big.

"Okay, I'll take it slowly. These pictures of the pets, naturally I'm curious. Why the interest?"

Helen came over to the cabinet and started looking them over. "Oh, let's just say I've always felt my own connection to the presidential pets. If they could talk, they'd tell you some stories."

"Yes, some of them are cute," I agreed.

"That's one way of putting it," she answered curtly. She caught herself and spoke more gently. "Look at the Kennedys here." She showed me a picture of Jack and Jackie with Caroline and John-

John, tanned, healthy, and happy, with Charlie the Welsh terrier and Pushinka the beautiful white half husky. Pushinka was a gift to Jackie from Soviet premier Khrushchev and the daughter of the famed space dog Strelka.

Helen probably had especially fond memories of the Kennedy administration. She was a brand-new White House reporter back in 1961, full of ambition. Although she was restricted to covering Jackie (that was a "woman's beat"), her memories of the Camelot period were bound to be extra sweet. "Those dogs were special," she said meaningfully.

"Oh, I'm sure they were lots of fun." It was a lovely picture.

"I don't think you're getting me." She looked hard at me. "Sit down." I sat. She opened a drawer, pulled out a manuscript, and tossed it on my lap. It was an edited draft for a magazine piece that she'd written. Right off the bat the title was crossed out.

~~`"'The Cuban Missile Crisis: The Honest to Dog Truth,'`~~ by Helen Thomas, *Ladies' Home Journal*. First draft, October 29, 1962," the headline read. That was the day after the tensest thirteen days in American history came to a close. I looked up at Helen.

"Don't stop now," she said.

9

How the Pupniks Saved
Civilization

As a rookie gal reporter in our nation's capital, there's no place more exciting to cover than the White House, home of our Commander-in-Chief. Recent events have had all of us feeling a bit on edge but that hasn't stopped Mrs. Kennedy from continuing her stunning restoration of the presidential mansion. Already it's come a long way since the days when Abigail Adams hung laundry in the East Room.

Last year the First Lady invited me to follow her around during a series of visits spanning eighteen months. The first took place in April of 1961. Mrs. Kennedy's press secretary, Miss Letitia Baldrige, led me to the beautifully refurbished elliptical Blue Room, where I waited for the First Lady, who was understandably delayed by the innumerable obligations that come with her position as Chief Hostess.

With a spectacular view of the South Lawn, the French Empire Blue Room, with its suite of gilded furniture and marble-top center table, was the site of Grover Cleveland's 1886 exchange of wedding vows with the beautiful Frances Folsom, and an appropriate place for cooling my heels. The Clevelands were the last couple before the Kennedys to raise small children in the White House and the oh-so-precious gold-plated miniature carousel I found there, a gift from Charles de Gaulle, demonstrated that it is indeed a long way from Cleveland to Camelot!

Mrs. Kennedy rushed in, flush with excitement and trailed by her dashing friend and designer to the stars, Oleg Cassini. Mrs. Kennedy, as entrancing as the photographs suggest, and Mr. Cassini were accompanied by a short Spanish man with a cello case, all three weighed down with shopping bags from all the best boutiques.

"Miss Thomas, please forgive me! Saks is a terrible labyrinth. But Oleg and I have conceived of the most *new* look for me today. It's really too exciting. Oh pardon me, have you met world-famous cellist Pablo Casals?" The cellist greeted me warmly. "Senor Casals joined us for espresso. I insisted he stay on." Mrs. Kennedy's White House is indeed a salon to rival any in Europe.

Just then a beautiful white dog, part husky, pulled up the rear.

"Oh, and you must say hello to Pushinka, the latest addition to the family." The recent gift from Soviet premier Khrushchev to Mrs. Kennedy of Pushinka, the daughter of pioneering space dog Strelka, was rumored to have been a source of some disagreement between the President and First Lady. Dare I ask?

"Oh, the President is a man and any man can be incorrigible."

Just then the President himself came in, trailed by his Welsh terrier Charlie, a fine-looking dog with the swagger of a young Bill Holden. The President greeted the First Lady: ~~"Jackie, have you seen my corticosteroids? Damned Addison's is flaring up again." Almost an afterthought,~~ the President smiled ~~tightly~~ at Mr. Cassini, Mr. Casals, and yours truly. Mr. Cassini gave an extravagant bow.

~~"I'm sorry, Jack, I haven't," said Mrs. Kennedy, then under her breath added, "It wouldn't hurt to smile at Pushinka. She's such a sweetie."~~

~~The President responded in a similarly hushed tone. "We've been through this before, Jackie. You cannot accept gifts from the enemy and expect me to be happy about it. We're in a Cold *War*, I've got a Bay of Pigs fiasco on my hands, *and* I'm out of Lomotil!"~~

~~Naturally the rest of us pretended not to hear this heated exchange. I turned to the dog in question and she said to me, in quite a thick Russian accent, "Stupid Americans." I was the only one who heard. I must say I was surprised by Pushinka's outspokenness—and the President's.~~

~~"Pushinka can stay as long as she checks out with the doctors at Walter Reed," said the President.~~

~~"But, Jack, she doesn't need a doctor. She's in perfectly good health. Why, if she were a horse, I'd fit her with a bridle this very instant!"~~ Mrs. Kennedy did look particularly smart in jodhpurs.

~~"Jackie, we can't mess with security. She could very well be bugged by the KGB."~~

~~Pushinka turned back to me and banged her paw on the floor indignantly. " 'Bugged'? I am certainly cleaner than American dog."~~

Secretary of Defense Bob McNamara suddenly poked his head in the door. "Mr. President, we've got a ~~Bay of Pigs Fiasco~~ meeting in ten minutes. ~~The Joint Chiefs are losing patience with you."~~

"And I've got to meet Balenciaga at four!" exclaimed Mrs. Kennedy, suddenly noticing her watch. The White House is indeed a very busy place.

On my next visit Mrs. Kennedy showed me the wonderful work she'd done on the Red Room, the more intimate space favored by another great hostess, First Lady Dolley Madison, for her Wednesday night receptions. The walls are covered in a red twill fabric with a gold scroll design in the borders, the furniture upholstered in a silk of the same shade.

Joining the First Lady today were the poet Robert Frost and the artist Ben Shahn. And in a kind of inauguration for the room, Rudolf Nureyev had accepted Mrs. Kennedy's invitation to dance for her.

Mr. Nureyev had only just begun pirouetting when the President entered ~~in his still-wet swimming trunks, looking for a painkiller for his abscess. "I was just splashing around with Fiddle and Faddle when it started acting up. Dr. Feelgood says I need a shot of procaine and some~~

phenobarbital." I took this opportunity to slip out and do some exploring on my own.

Up in the glorious Solarium former ambassador Joseph Kennedy Sr., a tumbler of Scotch in one hand, was sitting in front of the TV, nodding off. This sunny room is a cozy place for the First Family to gather and watch TV. Ambassador Kennedy was watching a Gloria Swanson film marathon.

Next to Ambassador Kennedy Pushinka and her new pal Charlie the terrier sat on the floor, snuggled awfully closely. Inquiring minds want to know.

"At first I hate him," confessed Pushinka. "I think him stupid. Like American government who make me have X-ray." Pushinka had been cleared of espionage aspirations. "I really don't understand him at beginning."

Charlie looked on adoringly. "I called her a riddle wrapped in a mystery inside a very cold kennel."

"I call him pygmy like Premier Khrushchev call President Kennedy. Then one day he put on Mrs. Kennedy's pillbox hat and dance for me." She laughed, then turned wistful. "In Mother Russia we love the burlesque." Charlie drew her closer.

But don't current international politics make their relationship difficult?

"Pushinka and I believe that we can do our part to show that this Cold War is pointless," said Charlie. "After all, only pit bulls like Air Force General Curtis LeMay would want to destroy each other. If that man is capable of love, it must be a very strange love.

"We will remind them of what ordinary people

want." Pushinka was passionate. "Unless of course we are doomed from start," she added, with a sudden far-off look in her eyes. "Oh, I want to go to Moscow."

Charlie laughed. "That's my Russkie. Too much Chekhov and not enough Chaplin."

They are a wonderful couple.

Mrs. Kennedy burst in with her friends Vogue editrix Diana Vreeland and step-cousin Gore Vidal, both of whom had just dropped in to say hi. "Miss Thomas, I'd wondered where you'd gone off to!" she chirped. "Don't you just love the Solarium?"

It was a gorgeous setting.

"I'm so glad you like it," she continued. "Now I'm afraid I must run. I'm hosting a state dinner for the Queen of Thailand. Oleg!" she cried, rushing out.

There's never a dull day for America's First Lady.

My most recent visit to the White House was October 28. The nation was on high alert after the discovery of Soviet missiles in Cuba. A naval blockade of the island had been in place for seven days, yet Soviet carriers had not changed their course. We all feared the end might be near.

Mrs. Kennedy had arranged an exquisite luncheon and tour of the refurbished West Wing for her dear friends Norman Mailer and Marcel Marceau. It promised to be a lovely occasion.

Mrs. Kennedy is that winning combination of glamorous and prudent. "When we enter the Oval

Office we should probably keep our voices down. The President and his advisors are trying to concentrate."

"Pardon me, folks," came a voice from behind as we made the approach to the most important office in America. It was none other than Vice President Lyndon Johnson. ~~He'd just been to the pharmacy to pick up a prescription of Trasentine for the President's chronic diarrhea.~~ "Forgive me for bargin' through. The President needs me right fast," ~~then added under his breath, "Son of a bitch spavined hunchback should find someone else to git him his dope."~~

Just outside the door, nestled in a box on the floor, was my old friend Pushinka. Charlie was standing guard over her. It seemed like they were up to something.

We entered the Oval Office and found the President at work, ~~surrounded by his top advisors, also known as the ExCommers, civilians and military men sharply divided on the question of how to proceed: continue the blockade or attack Cuba.~~

~~"I've got two letters from Khrushchev here, men," said the President, his handsome face slightly marred by the emergence of several painful-looking sores. "In one, he's playing nice, he wants to make a deal. In the other he's picking a fight. Which do I respond to?"~~

~~"Mr. President, we really don't want to fight, do we?" counseled the professorial UN Ambassador Adlai Stevenson. "Respond to the first missive and maintain the blockade."~~

~~"Shut up, egghead," snapped Air Force General LeMay. "It's really pretty clear, Mr. President.~~

You gotta fry 'em or you're gonna look like a coward and we'll have another Munich on our hands. So just give the word and we'll get cooking."

"Blockade them, I say!" said Stevenson.

"Firebomb 'em back to the Stone Age!" said LeMay.

"Blockade!"

"Fry 'em!"

While this heated discussion went on, Mrs. Kennedy pointed out the desk, a gift from Queen Victoria to President Hayes, built from the timbers of the HMS *Resolute*. Quite an impressive piece. While Mrs. Kennedy described the presidential seal on the ceiling of the office, I slipped back into the hall to visit with my canine friends.

Pushinka didn't look well. And Charlie was in distress. "Tell me she's going to be okay," he said to me.

Pushinka moaned. "Charlie, what is happening is natural."

From the other room, we could hear the President growing more desperate. "Bobby, what should I do?"

"Jack, I don't know. The generals do have a point. I mean, that Bay of Pigs really was a fiasco. But this time you have to take responsibility."

"It really does afford a gorgeous view of the Rose Garden," Mrs. Kennedy said to her guests.

"I'm hungry for some huevos rancheros! FRY 'EM!!" screamed LeMay.

Pushinka turned to me, "Miss Thomas, hand me forceps. We cannot wait a second longer." I

~~handed her a pair of salad tongs that she must have smuggled from the kitchen. Charlie turned away as the miracle of life began unfolding.~~

~~"Bobby," said a nervous President from the other room. "Write down the following message for Ambassador Dobrynin to carry to the Premier . . ."~~

Just then Mrs. Kennedy breezed back into the hallway, took one look at Pushinka's handiwork, and exclaimed, "Puppies!" Indeed Pushinka had just given birth. We were all in a state of delighted shock. Marcel Marceau's mouth was in a perfectly formed circle, his hands up by his face to signify astonishment.

The President's advisors quickly gathered round, followed by the President himself. Before them, huddled together were proud parents Charlie and Pushinka and their four newborns. Everyone tried to move closer but Marcel Marceau used his hands to cordon off the area around the new family, ~~so that Pushinka could eat her placenta in peace.~~

~~The President was moved. "Do you mean to tell me that my American dog fell in love with that Soviet dog and they went and had kids?!"~~

Mrs. Kennedy had tears in her eyes. "It's true. They're a brand-new family. Oh, Jack, now it's settled. We *must* include the doghouse in our restoration. I'm seeing something in Veronese green!"

The President shook his head, moved by the scene before him. ~~"So maybe the Russians and we aren't so different. Gosh, I'm feeling something I haven't felt for a long time."~~

~~"Uh-oh, I hope it's not your tinnitus acting up again," said Bobby.~~

~~"No, Bobby, I've got Librium for that. It's something different."~~

~~"I know what it is," said McNamara. "It's empathy."~~

~~"Empathy for the enemy," said President Kennedy, looking at the pupniks' mother. "Sorry, General LeMay, I'm going to choose the *sane* option and make a deal with the Soviets." The President looked down at the puppies. "These little pupniks deserve it."~~

~~Then the President pulled a vial from his pocket and raised it. "Testosterone for everyone!" he toasted as everyone except the Joint Chiefs cheered. Marcel Marceau mime-clapped. General LeMay punched him.~~

"Now if you'll excuse me," said the President, "I've got some work to do." The President, gracious as always, went back into his office ~~and resumed his dictation. "Bobby, take this down: We'll guarantee that we won't attack Cuba and we'll even pull those missiles out of Turkey so that he can save face. But the Premier's got to pull out of Cuba completely . . ."~~

The thirteen stressful days of October will never be forgotten. Many believe that things turned out peacefully because the President and his staff had such a wonderful environment in which to resolve the conflict, thanks to Mrs. John F. Kennedy. ~~The truth, however, is that Pushinka and Charlie—and Butterfly, White Tips, Blackie, and Streaker—reminded an isolated President of the potential costs of a decision that~~

Kennedy dogs Charlie and Pushinka. Their "negotiations" averted a nuclear nightmare.

~~was ultimately his and his alone—and in doing so~~
~~saved the planet from an unspeakable fate.~~

Helen saw that I'd finished reading. "Pretty interesting, huh? Sometime I'll tell you how Caroline's pony, Macaroni, helped write the Atmospheric Test Ban Treaty."

I didn't really hear her. I was floored by what I'd read, but not by the talking animals. I assumed this was some Orwell-for-kids rhetorical device employed by an overly experimental young reporter. It didn't surprise me that the animals' "words" had been blacked out by Helen's editor. Some readers might have actually thought Helen was being literal.

What concerned me more was how very close we'd come to Armageddon. The edited version didn't convey that. "Why wasn't this published, Helen?" I asked.

She averted her eyes from mine. "It just wouldn't have been appropriate. There were other priorities—like Mrs. Kennedy's fall collection '62, which really did change the way we all thought about empire waists and formal gloves," she said, more than a little bit defensively.

"Well it's a good thing this is documented. Someone should know this."

"Yes, that is important." Then she looked deeply into my eyes. "There's so much to tell and it's very important that someone know it."

I was more than happy to be the repository for Helen's collected wisdom. "I'm fascinated, Helen. I want to know it all." A rustling sound from the dark beyond the bookcases broke the tension. Helen began shooing me away.

"You should go now. We'll have plenty more time to talk." She opened the entranceway and pushed me out. "There's a shortcut out onto 17th Street. Climb halfway up the stairs, then follow the tunnel on your right. It will lead you up through a manhole in front of the Old Executive Office Building."

I did exactly as directed. It was a tight and smelly squeeze—and it was blocked at the top by an ice cream truck. I waited till the sun had fallen and the truck had moved to push out the manhole, then hoisted myself up and onto the street. A D.C. cop noticed me climbing out.

"Hey you! What do you think you're doing, climbing out a manhole next to the White House? We're under orange-level alert right now."

"Actually," I stammered, "it's only yellow alert right now."

"Oh, that's right. Sorry to bother you."

I was off to the Outback.

10

The Alien and Sedition Acts, *or* How I Went to the Outback Steakhouse with Coulter, Crowley, Hannity and Colmes and Almost Lost My Mind

"Jesus, you smell!" bellowed Candy as I slid in on her side of the booth at Outback. "You been swimming in the sewers or something?"

"You could call it that." I'd barely had a minute to wipe off.

"Hey, Miss Joe McCoulter, lemme bum another butt," said Candy. "Anything to overpower the stench over here." Ann Coulter sat on the other side, squeezed between Sean Hannity and Alan Colmes. She'd nearly filled her saucer-turned-ashtray to the brim and she was still puffing away. A copy of her latest best seller, *Sedition*—the last in her "Love It or Leave It" trilogy—was on the table.

"You remember Ann, don't you, Mo?" Candy asked as Ann gave her a cig.

"Of course I do." I had met Ann on several occasions. She was a lightning rod, someone who believed more than half of what she said, remarkable by Washington standards. She was also a lot of fun, if you could keep her off politics. "How are you?"

"Fine, Mo, fine. I'm just trying to explain to our Clintonista pal over there"—she gestured to Candy—"and this little bozo over here"—she elbowed Colmes; he smiled awkwardly—"that Mussolini in fact was very funny. It's all in my book. And seriously, Candy, I challenge you to find annotated proof anywhere that Mussolini was never in fact charming."

"Christ, Ann, maybe we should be eating somewhere where you can order Chicken Pol Pot."

"No, Candy, NO." Ann was becoming agitated. "The fact of the matter was that Pol Pot was a dickless son of a bitch. A complete and total pussy who let the Vietnamese drive him off course, not surprising since he was an extremist *Liberal.* So don't give me that shit."

"That's my girl," Hannity said, his arm around Ann. Ann nearly swallowed her cigarette, she was so worked up.

I had to intervene. "Guys, I know I just got here but can't we just relax?"

Colmes spoke up ever so softly and haltingly. "I think that Mo has made a very good point."

"Shut your pie hole!" Ann snapped at him. He winced. She then turned to me. "You're absolutely right, Mo. Let's talk about you," she said, surprisingly sweetly. "Haven't seen you in ages. I'm so glad you're off that Traficant show. What a communist."

"Jim was many things, I'm just not sure he was a communist. But I appreciate it. I'm happier now."

"Cool beans," said Ann.

An earthy but attractive waitress with a "Free Saddam, Hunt Down Bush" T-shirt and John Kerry for President button approached us. Hannity instinctively stuck out his chest. The waitress didn't notice. "Excuse me, you two. But the restaurant has a strict no-smoking policy."

"Then I'm going to stop killing myself right this instant," said Candy, who put out her cigarette in the saucer and popped a

Nicorette. Ann looked straight ahead and defiantly took another drag on her cigarette. The waitress wasn't cowed.

"Miss, it's a no-smoking policy. No exception."

Ann turned to her with the fakest smile she could muster. "I'm so sorry, sweetie. I must not have heard you, hon." She placed the cigarette in the saucer, then exaggeratedly slapped her hands against each other, as if she were finished with her dirty work. "All done!" she grinned with a mock-girlish enthusiasm.

The waitress's eye roll was a giveaway that she recognized Ann. She left, shaking her head.

Ann dropped the Shirley Temple act instantly. "John Kerry for President," she scoffed. "Commander-in-Chief?! Dammit, I'm embarrassed to have a vagina." She picked the still-lit cigarette up and ostentatiously resumed puffing. "You realize that that little slut is a living breathing example of sedition, don't you?" As Ann finished her cigarette, Colmes was waiting with one freshly lit by him.

"Ann, I agree that the T-shirt is a little much but sedition is a pretty serious—" I began.

"I'm not talking about the T-shirt, Mo. I'm talking about the Kerry button. Anyone conspiring to 'overthrow, put down, or destroy' the government of the United States is guilty of sedition. And that's what the Kerry voters want—to put down this government."

"Yes, by *voting* it out," I said. I could only accommodate her so much.

Ann shook her head hard and kept puffing. "Voting it out, putting it down, what's the difference? It's still sedition. And according to Title 18, Section 2384 of the United States Law—which I, for your information, did not make up—it is *outlawed*. The only thing I'd change is I'd make it punishable by death."

This got a rise out of Candy. "Death? Christ, Ann, you want everyone who votes for a Democrat to be put to death?"

ANN COULTER

AUTHOR OF THE #1 NATIONAL BESTSELLER *TREASON*

SEDITION

WHY VOTING FOR A DEMOCRAT
SHOULD BE PUNISHABLE BY DEATH

"If that's what it takes to make this country safe again, then yes, Candy. Because guess what? *I* happen to love my country." Ann was puffing so hard, she was shrouded in a cloud of white smoke. That's when the waitress returned, looking none too pleased.

"Uh-oh, here we go," sighed Candy, resigned to yet another Coulter spectacle. I had never witnessed one of Ann's famed knock-down drag-outs in person. On TV she would stake a claim that even her staunchest partisans were afraid to take and she'd do a surprisingly good job of defending herself. Smoking at the Outback seemed smaller stakes than the legacy of the Red Scare, though.

The waitress wasted no time getting personal. "Miss, I guess I'm surprised that you of all people are not understanding some basic law and order here." She glanced down at the copy of *Sedition*. "Maybe you should be carrying a dictionary. 'Prohibited' means 'against the law.' "

The battle lines were drawn. Ann was facing an unambiguously smug opponent. Suddenly she was Dick Nixon staring down the haughty East Coast establishment. She wasn't going to skulk away to some backroom to plot revenge, then deny responsibility, though. A liberal Democrat with balls, a threat to national security, was standing in her crosshairs. It was time to unload a bunker buster.

"Thanks for the explanation, Justice Ruth Bader Lezbo, but guess what?" she taunted. "It's not a law. A *rule,* yes," she puffed on her cigarette, "but not a law." Hannity snickered. Colmes looked terrified—and aroused.

The waitress laughed. "You actually think that insulting me is going to work?"

"Oh, sweetie, don't take what I say so seriously. I'm sure you've laid all kinds of dirtbags in your day. You know, we should get you down to Gitmo. The prisoners down there would love a whore like you."

I had to say something. "Ann, can we please go someplace else? I think it's a little unfair to expect the restaurant to let us smoke." I used "us" because, frankly, I was too scared to challenge her directly.

"Fine. Let me put this out first." For a split second, I thought Ann had come to her senses and backed down—until she suddenly grabbed the waitress's right wrist and began grinding the cigarette into her hand! The waitress shrieked.

"Holy shit, Ann! You've lost your mind!" screamed Candy.

I reached across the table and pushed Ann against the banquette, away from the waitress. The waitress managed to wrest away her hand. She looked at the burn with wide-eyed horror, then narrowed her eyes at Ann.

"You fascist bitch," she snarled.

"You can do better than that," Ann laughed, then took another puff off her weapon and exhaled. "Bring it on."

The waitress leaped forward and started strangling Ann. Ann was unfazed. The cigarette still dangled from her lips.

"Smoking! . . . Is! . . . PROHIBITED!" raged the now unhinged waitress, tightening her grip. The best I could do was try to pull the waitress from behind but years of hiking and gorp consumption had made her strong as an ox. Only Hannity and Colmes were in a position to help stop the madness but they seemed paralyzed.

"Playtime's over," said Candy, who opened her purse and reached for her pearl-handled revolver.

"Candy, no," I snapped. "That's not the answer."

Candy crossed her arms and sat back. "I tried."

Meanwhile Ann was turning beet red, eyes bulging, her body trembling from the lack of oxygen as the waitress gripped harder. Like the flag at Iwo Jima, though, the cigarette was still there. This could well be her last breath and she knew what to say.

"From . . . my . . . cold . . . dead . . . hands." Other restaurant patrons had gathered round and began screaming—a couple of them even tried to help me, to little avail. Then with her trembling left arm Ann felt her way around the Bloomin' Onion to a bottle of Corona. She carefully lifted it up and smashed it over Colmes's head, creating a jagged weapon. Before she could plunge it into her enemy's face, the waitress came to her senses and jumped back.

"Are you fucking crazy?" she asked. It was a reasonable question.

Ann shook her head, amused. "Democrats. Always weak on defense." She took a sip of water, stood up, and hobbled out of the restaurant still puffing away.

Hannity was halfheartedly holding a wadded-up napkin against Colmes's profusely bleeding head wound. "I'm sorry for bleeding on the tablecloth, Sean," stammered Colmes. Hannity wasn't listening but looking off in Ann's direction. "She's going to go hook up with Drudge, I know it," he muttered desperately before giving his ailing cohost one last look. "Sorry, guy." He instantly let the napkin drop and chased after Ann. "Hey, Ann, wait up!"

It all seemed so surreal. I turned to Candy.

"Politics," she shrugged, then turned to the waitress. "Could you wrap up the rest of the onion?"

11

Federalist Smackdown

"Take a deep breath. You're hysterical," Helen said.

I'd made my way back to her lair; I'm not sure why. Something told me she'd give me perspective. But first I needed to be talked down. I was hyperventilating.

"And Ann was so angry and Candy had a gun and the waitress's flesh was burning and Colmes was just bleeding everywhere." My voice started to crack. "Oh, Helen—"

Helen pulled my head to her breast and dabbed it with a cold compress. "There, there, Colmes'll be fine. The truth is, he likes getting roughed up. That's his job." Helen was so motherly and I didn't want to reject her, but pressed up against her like that, my nose immediately began itching. Was there a cat somewhere? I backed off as I let out a big sneeze.

"Bless you, dear!" Helen exclaimed.

"Pardon me. Anyway, Helen, I couldn't believe the disgusting display. I can appreciate people disagreeing but it was so uncivil, so deeply personal. Violently *personal*. Maybe I'm sounding naive."

"You're sounding naive. If I've learned anything about Washington culture, it is that it's about extremes. On the one hand you've got the cocktail party set who like to make nicey-nice. With them you can't tell the difference between a San Francisco Socialist and a Birmingham Bible Belter. Then you've got the true believers, also known as the Screamers. The problem with them is they don't just believe they know the truth. They *know* they know the truth."

"Okay, you can call me a drip, but why can't anyone just talk calmly, honestly—and substantively? I'm sure that the Founding Fathers would be appalled—"

"Darling, you're sounding like a drip. You don't think the Founding Fathers could go on the attack? They were the ones who started all this partisan nonsense. Sure, there were a few who tried to keep discourse on a higher level. President Washington was pretty 'dignified'—which is a nice way of saying he was boring," she added under her breath.

"Boring?"

"Oh, please. The man's biography was written by a guy named Parson Weems. Jefferson on the other hand? What a life. Kitty Kelley would have gone to town. But I digress. Washington didn't like conflict and more than anything he feared the creation of parties. But the minute he was out and back at Mount Vernon, battle lines were drawn. That's not to say there weren't some calmer voices of reason."

With that Helen opened up her file and handed me a scrolled-up sheet of parchment. I unfurled it. The title of the document—it appeared to be a transcript of some kind of discussion—written out in calligraphy, read "A crossfire of opinions concerning the Alien and Sedition Acts."

I only had a workingman's knowledge of the Alien and Sedition Acts, which were the most serious restrictions on freedom of expression ever passed by Congress. Hotly debated in the press, the most infamous of the four articles, the Sedition Act, included a $2,000 fine and imprisonment for "writing, printing, uttering or publishing any false, scandalous and malicious writing" against the President or Congress. Passed by a Federalist-controlled Congress purportedly in response to the hostile behavior of the French Revolutionary government, the acts inflamed allies of Thomas Jefferson and precipitated the creation of the party system in American politics, setting the stage for the electoral revolution of 1800.

At least that was my vague recollection.

The scroll was dated 1798, the second year of John Adams's administration. The names Toddy the bulldog and Buzzy the Briard sheepdog were included below the title.

"Toddy the bulldog belonged to John Adams," I said, a little uneasy. "And Buzzy was the dog that Jefferson brought back from Paris."

"So tell me something I don't know," Helen said flatly. I read on.

October 1, 1798
Tonight!
A CROSSFIRE
of opinions concerning
The Alien and Sedition Acts
To be debated this even in Rittenhouse Town Square
On the Federalist side, Toddy the Bulldog.
On the Jeffersonian Republican side,
Buzzy the Briard Sheepdog.
Wassail to be served.

TOWN CRIER: Come one, come all to witness the Crossfire!

TODDY: Good evening and welcome to our crossfire, an

opportunity to exchange ideas in the hopes of edify-
ing ourselves and the public, all in the service of
better governance. On the Federalist side I'm Toddy
the bulldog.

BUZZY: And on the Jeffersonian Republican side, I'm
Buzzy the sheepdog. The Federalist-controlled Congress
has just passed four articles known as the Alien and
Sedition Acts. Are the acts an unnecessary curb on free
speech?

TODDY: Or are they simply meant to protect this young
fragile nation against foreign hostilities and the
anarchy of the recent French Revolution? Joining us to
explore these questions are, on my worthy opponent's
side, bestselling author of the Constitution, Mr. James
Madison.

BUZZY: And on my respected colleague's side, architect of our financial system and former aide-de-camp to
Washington, Mr. Alexander Hamilton.

TODDY: Mr. Madison, let's start with you. Can you see
any merit in the argument that the national government
may need some protection from potentially subversive
elements?

MADISON: Look, Toddy, let's cut to the chase here.
Your retro-royalist plot to strip Americans of their
newly enshrined individual rights and bigfoot the rest
of us with your overbearing London-loving central government is totally transparent. So the only thing I have
to say to you is, Shame on you, Toddy the English bulldog, shame on you.

TODDY: Actually I'm an *American* Bulldog but I—

ALEXANDER HAMILTON: Can I get a word in edgewise? Let
me explain something to our wine-swilling Limoges-
lusting France-First friends across the aisle. While
you stroll around the plantation, philosophizing about
America as some weirdo agrarian utopia, the rest of us
are busy building an industrial base and protecting ourselves from enemies. So I guess my question for Buzzy
and Mr. Madison is, why do you hate America so much?

BUZZY: Mr. Hamilton, I don't hate—

MADISON: Get yourself some new talking points, Hamilton. Neither of us is going to be put down by the hardball tactics you and your Federalist cronies consistently enlist in trying to subvert my Constitution.

HAMILTON: *Your* Constitution? The last time I checked I wrote fifty-two of the Federalist Papers in support of its ratification. You wrote how many?

(Silence.)

MADISON: I'm not going to respond.

HAMILTON: How many?

MADISON: I'm not taking the bait again.

HAMILTON: Twenty-six, is it?

MADISON: Twenty-eight!!

HAMILTON: Oooh, big man with twenty-eight Federalist Papers under his belt. I'm sooo impressed.

MADISON: You know, Hamilton, you're not just a bastard. You're a total arsehole.

HAMILTON: Hey, I'd rather be an arsehole than have my lips locked around Jefferson's codger 24/7!

MADISON: I hope you get shot.

BUZZY: Mr. Hamilton, Mr. Madison, please!! Can we stick to the issues?

MADISON: He started it.

HAMILTON: Sorry, but the numbers don't lie. It's twenty-six, right?

MADISON: Twenty-eight!!

TODDY: Enough, gentlemen. Now, Buzzy, here's the way I see it: The President *may* have reason to be nervous about France or any other foreign power who might benefit from discord in this country.

BUZZY: Yes, Toddy, national security is of the utmost importance but I really don't think criticizing our government is going to make France more likely to invade us. My fear is that the Federalist Party may want these acts signed into law so that they can consolidate power and avoid any criticism at all.

TODDY: Buzzy, that's an absolutely valid concern and one that I'll bring to President Adams's attention. But grant that an unfettered freedom to criticize the government does smack of mob rule. And who trusts a mob?

BUZZY: I certainly don't. But trying to suppress a "mob" is only going to create more dissent.

TODDY: True, true.

BUZZY: People will only want more freedom more quickly. Besides, inevitably this Republic will become a true democracy as more people are given the right to vote.

TODDY: I certainly concede that point. But until then how do we balance security concerns with liberty?

BUZZY: Well, I think we should agree that *treasonous* acts are outlawed—acts of deliberate betrayal against the government, rather than written words that purportedly incite rebellion.

TODDY: That, my friend, sounds like a fair compromise. We certainly don't want to violate a central freedom we just fought so hard to safeguard. It would be too too ironic. I think we should also engage the French and English in strict policies of neutrality to minimize threats from overseas.

BUZZY: Good point. That is what President Washington advised us in his Farewell Address.

TODDY: Then it's settled. Now this has been a very fruitful discussion. Mr. Hamilton, what do you think? Mr. Hamilton?

BUZZY: Mr. Hamilton?

HAMILTON: Was someone talking?

BUZZY: Well, yes. We were just having what I think was a productive discussion.

HAMILTON: That's great because I was just having what I think was a productive naptime.

BUZZY: Mr. Madison, do you have any thoughts?

MADISON: Yes. First of all, this show is in trouble. You're doing it all wrong.

TODDY: How would you prefer we behave?

MADISON: Oh, I don't know. Like dogs? Call Buzzy a mongrel.

HAMILTON: Maybe bite him.

MADISON: At least bark.

HAMILTON: There's more barking on *The Burr Factor* and they just have one host. No wonder more people show up at their town square.

MADISON: You should try to rip his throat out.

(Hamilton laughs.)

MADISON: What's so funny?

HAMILTON: I'm trying to imagine you ripping someone's throat out. How tall are you? Twenty-six inches?

MADISON: Twenty-eight!!!

(Madison lunges at Hamilton.)

BUZZY: Oh dear.

TODDY: Please join us tomorrow when our guests will discuss this year's wedge issue, the three-fifths clause of the Constitution.

It was quite a read. The hosts were so cordial and the guest debaters were like animals.

But of course this was all fiction. Who knew that the leading lady of the American press corps was a closet short-story writer?

"How did you make it look so old?" I asked, referring to the wrinkled scroll.

"I didn't. Two hundred-plus years will do that to a piece of paper."

"So this is original. It just happens to include two dogs. Helen, do you really expect me—?"

But before I finished the question, I heard Wolf Blitzer's voice in my head. "Mo-san, you must keep an open mind. And believe." Wolf had never actually said those words but they seemed like words he would have said if confronted with a scene like this.

Helen was pondering the scroll. "It might interest you to know that Toddy ended up advising President Adams to veto the legislation. But Adams chickened out. He was too afraid of what his 'supporters' in the Federalist Party would do if he didn't sign it. So he signed it. Then he tried to make it up to the Virginians by making peace with the French and talking a lot about individual liberty. Poor guy tried so hard to stay in the middle of the road he got run over," Helen said, adding cryptically, "not that there's anything wrong with roadkill."

"Yes, Adams got devoured by the party system," I said. "Only Washington was strong enough to remain above party division."

"Then in came Jefferson, our first partisan President," said Helen.

"So whatever happened to that run of Crossfire?" I asked.

"It did well for a while and played most of the town squares in prime time before it started getting very very shouty. At first that excited people. But by the time Monroe was President people had turned against it. All they wanted to watch were minstrel shows. Lord, that was a vapid time."

"You're referring to the Era of Good Feelings," I said.

" 'Good Feelings'?" Helen shook her head. "Everyone acted like they were on Prozac. Monroe ended up running unopposed in 1824."

Helen did have a point there. The only thing worse than a stupid debate was no debate.

But I still had a question about the Alien and Sedition Acts. "After all was said and done, do you really think Hamilton believed those acts were justified?"

Helen laughed. "He rails against the dangers of sedition, then three years later he starts the *New York Post.*" She pointed to a yellowed clipping on her wall.

"They had Page Six back then?"

"And it was actually on the sixth page," Helen added. "Life was so much simpler."

A blind item from this Page Six caught my eye. It read: "Which strapping redhead has declared his own independence from conventional standards and taken on a new housebound gal pal?"

"My God, is that a reference to President Jefferson and—"

"—Sally Hemings. Yes, it was the first mention."

I wanted to hear more but it was getting late, and tomorrow was a big day for me. President Bush was meeting with President Vicente Fox of Mexico. Immigration would be the major issue of discussion. Of course there would be no formal press conference. (The President had held a record few of those.) There would be a photo op, though, where the press would have a chance to scream a few questions.

"Just get in there and make yourself heard," advised Helen.

That I could do. But as usual, trying to address any real issue, couched in the language of my peculiar beat, was going to be difficult. President McKinley had a Mexican yellow-headed parrot named Washington Post that used to whistle at women and say, "Oh, look at all the pretty girls."

"Maybe that could be my way in," I said.

"Sounds like a conversation stopper to me," snapped Helen. "If you want some real background on the immigration issue, meditate on this."

Once again Helen had her own reading recommendation. It seemed I'd befriended an amateur librarian—one with a particularly strange fetish, in this case talking-animal lit. Yes, the cover of the volume she pulled from one of her shelves featured another quadruped, this time a Siamese cat. *Miss Pussy and the President,* the title read. Apparently it had nothing to do with

President Clinton. In fact the cover illustration looked like the art Sir John Tenniel created for *Alice's Adventures in Wonderland*.

"This looks like a children's book," I said.

"It *is* a children's book. I wrote it."

"Helen, that's really cool! When are you being published?"

"I *was* published. It didn't sell very well," she sighed, before glancing up coquettishly. "But it's a terrific story . . . wanna hear it?"

"Uh, sure."

I guess I asked for it.

12

Thai Me Up, Thai Me Down

Helen came alive. "Sit back, relax, and enjoy the show!" she commanded me. She insouciantly threw the book aside, pulled her Murphy bed out from the wall and pushed me onto it. Then she hopped onto her ottoman. For a moment I thought she might start singing "Let Me Entertain You" and do a striptease, but she'd said it was a children's story.

"Now you know about Rutherford B. Hayes and his wife, Lucy. Lucy was a strict woman." Helen threw on a black cloak to signify Lucy. "Very religious. No liquor in that White House."

"Right, they called her Lemonade Lucy," I said.

"Well, Lemonade Lucy had a whole bunch of pets. Mutts, pigeons, a goat. Real hillbilly pets. Lucy had taken them all in from the street, cleaned them up, and taught them to sing church hymns like 'Rock of Ages.' But when they were alone they'd start jamming!"

Helen tossed off the cloak and started imitating the animals singing Stephen Foster in an exaggerated "redneck" voice:

I said, Oh, Susannah
Now don't you cry for me

ALL THE PRESIDENTS' PETS

As I come from Alabama
with a banjo on my knee . . .

She pulled out a Jew's harp and a set of spoons and started riffing. Helen wasn't holding back—she went to town on the washboard—and I was instantly hooked.

"Then what happened, Helen?!"

"Well, one day the animals are doing their thing, strumming and plucking away in the Green Room—the floor all covered in hay, tin cans rolling around—when suddenly the doors fly open and they hear this gong sound." Helen imitated the sound. "The animals stop what they're doing and go slack-jawed because standing right in the doorway is a cat. Now this wasn't an ordinary cat. She was slender, golden-colored, with perfectly matched dark paws and ears. And she was terribly mysterious."

Helen grabbed a fan and fluttered it in front of her to represent mystery.

" 'Hello,' " she purred in an over-the-top "Asian" accent, " 'I am Miss Pussy.' " Helen shifted flawlessly back to her rednecky Jim Nabors voice.

" 'Well, I'll be, I think she's Chineeeeese,' said the mutt with a banjo.

" 'I am Siamese!' said Miss Pussy proudly. 'But China and Siam both in Asia.' "

I was so engrossed in Helen's unfolding mad scene that I almost forgot that the Hayeses were in fact the recipients of America's first Siamese cat, a gift from David Sickles, the American consul to Siam. Presumably he was bucking for a better assignment. Helen continued.

"The American animals were naturally spellbound as the blue-eyed Miss Pussy slinked around the room. When she rubbed up against the goat, he stomped his foot wildly." Helen stomped her foot. "Miss Pussy purred." Helen purred, then spoke in her Miss Pussy voice.

Miss Pussy's Grand Entrance.

An illustration from Helen's children's book.

" 'I come by steamer from Bangkok to Hawaii to San Francisco. Many Chinese workers in San Francisco. They help build railroad. I take railroad to Washington.'

"Then one of the pigeons spoke up. 'Pardon our staring. It's that we done never seen a cat like you. You're like a tiger, but purty like.'

"Miss Pussy laughed." Helen gave a girlish laugh. " 'I am not so different from you when you know me. In Bangkok I meet teacher from England. She sing song I now sing for you.' "

Helen, as Miss Pussy, began sashaying around the room, as if she were a cat.

> *Getting to know you,*
>> *Getting to know all about you.*
> *Getting to like you,*
>> *Getting to hope you like me.*

Helen sounded great on this. She was totally in the zone. (I made a mental note to request "I Enjoy Being a Girl" from *Flower Drum Song* at a later time.) She continued.

"The animals were riveted as Miss Pussy sauntered this way and that. Then without warning she slipped into her native tongue."

Helen started singing in Thai!

> ทั้งนี้ เพื่อช่วยให้คุณนึกถึงบุคคลหรือทีมงานที่สมควรแก่การ
> เสนอชื่อ เมื่อคุณเสนอชื่อบุคคลหรือทีมงานใด

"Now don't ask how," said Helen, "but the other animals joined in.

> คุณต้องชี้แจงเหตุผลว่า บุคคลหรือทีมงานนั้น
> เป็นตัวอย่างในพฤติกรรมเหล่านั้นอย่างไร เราคาดหวังว่าจะ
> มีผู้ได้รับการเสนอชื่อมากมาย !

"Oh my God, Helen," I broke in. "How did that happen?"

"I said don't ask. Just go with it," snapped Helen, before resuming her narrator's voice.

"Months passed and Miss Pussy and the other pets became the best of friends. They taught her how to whittle. She taught them about spring rolls and fan dancing. 'You American pets so afraid to be sexy!'

"But Miss Pussy soon began worrying. She read that the economy in California had slowed down and Chinese workers were being blamed for stealing jobs. Some Chinese workers had been killed in riots. To make matters worse, Congress had just passed a ban on Chinese immigrants, the first ban on any group in U.S. history.

" 'What's eating at you, Miss Pussy?' asked the goat one wintry day.

" 'Your United States Congress. They want to keep out Chinese immigrants after ten thousand help build railroad for little money and many die. Without them, there be no train!'

" 'But I thought you said you weren't Chineeeese,' said the goat. 'So why do you care?'

" 'I am Siamese, but I have many Chinese friends. Besides, in such an increasingly interconnected world, we are less separated than ever by racial and ethnic classification.' "

(This line struck me as anachronistic, but I didn't want to interrupt Helen.)

"One of the mutts spoke next. 'Well, maybe President Hayes won't sign that there legislation, if you can convince him.' "

Helen's Miss Pussy suddenly turned dark. " 'I fear there is little time, mutt. You see, Miss Pussy not feel so good.' " Helen dramatically coughed, in character. She stumbled over to a chaise longue and collapsed on it. It was a turn I didn't expect and I found myself sitting on the very edge of the bed.

Helen continued, Camille-like. " 'Bangkok not so cold. Miss Pussy become sick.' " She coughed again.

" 'Maybe she just needs a shot of moonshine,' said the goat.

" 'Is too late for moonshiny,' " said Helen's Miss Pussy weakly. " 'I have only few moments left.' "

My eyes welled up as Helen zipped over to the other side of the room, grabbed her cloak, then reentered as Lucy Hayes.

" 'Lord in heaven, there's something grievously wrong with Miss Pussy!' said Mrs. Hayes, aghast at the scene. 'Rud, come at once!' she called to her husband, who was at that very moment meeting with anti-Chinese lobbyists in the Blue Room.

"President Hayes rushed in." Helen had a top hat ready for this part. " 'What is happening?' he asked.

"With the greatest effort Miss Pussy turned her head toward the President and spoke. 'Please, Mr. President, I have dying wish.'

"The President knelt down beside the bed, surrounded by the other pets. 'What is it, Miss Pussy?' he asked, grabbing her paw."

Helen, back on the chaise, was fading fast. " 'Mr. President, Chinese Exclusion Act is wrong. Please veto . . . in name of Miss Pussy.'

" 'Miss Pussy,' said one of the mutts. 'You can't die on us now. We was just getting to know you.' "

Helen, as Miss Pussy, smiled wanly. The lighting in the room mysteriously dimmed, and Helen was cast in a soft glowing beam. Then barely audibly she began: " 'Getting to know you . . . Getting to . . . know . . . all . . .' "

I sat on the edge of the bed, riveted. I'd already grown attached to Helen's cat character. I wanted her to live forever.

"Oh, Miss Pussy," I softly cried—but to no avail. Helen took one last breath, then shut her eyes tight, signifying the death of Miss P. The other pets continued humming the melody to the song.

Helen donned the top hat again and made one final statement as President Hayes. " 'We cannot forget this day. To honor Miss Pussy I am going to veto the Chinese Exclusion Act.' "

A mournful gong sounded, supported by a lovely string orchestra. The lights faded to black, then came back up. "The End," said Helen with a bow, clutching a bouquet of flowers. It was over.

"Think on that and you'll do just fine tomorrow," said Helen.

I was emotionally spent from Helen's bravura performance. She was better than Nicole Kidman in the "Spectacular Spectacular" scene from *Moulin Rouge*. Just how it would help me address the issue of immigration with President Bush I didn't know, though I was unlikely to forget it. I dabbed my eyes, then headed home to study up for tomorrow.

13

The Fox and the Pussy

The next morning the press corps were herded out through the West Wing colonnade and into the Rose Garden area. Security corralled us into a tight area next to where Presidents Bush and Fox would soon appear. I could barely breathe. Helen, in her wisdom, was skipping this event.

"Uh, 'scuse me. Please, like, stop pushing," Norah O'Donnell snapped.

Norah was always so sharp with me, and I couldn't quite understand why. "You know, Norah, we both work for the same company. You could be a little nicer."

"Uh, hello-o? Not. I'm NBC, you're *MS*NBC. Major diff, got it?" Ouch.

Behind me, John King was furiously scrubbing his hands and arms with Purell, an afternoon ritual. A sound man accidentally brushed his boom microphone across John's hair. "Makeup!" King screamed. Instantly someone was on hand to regroom him.

Up in front stood Laurie. She wore a gorgeous green and red print dress, in honor of the Mexican colors, and a bright paper flower in her hair. Needless to say she looked terrific.

The doors of the Oval Office finally opened and Scott and his press aides—including Gephardt the Albino—entered. The two presidents followed.

I'd never seen the President this close up before and I was impressed, not least because of his natural jocularity toward the press corps. Before the press op was officially started, he gave a shout out to most of them, one after the other: "Binky . . . Cooter . . . Shrek . . . Tuna . . . Grabbyhands . . . Stinky . . ." Each time a reporter's name was called you could feel the excitement. Campbell "Taco" Brown shrieked when her name was called. When David "Frenchy" Gregory and Terry "Wombat" Moran heard their nicknames, they butted chests in celebration. I was hoping I might get a nickname, but serious business began before the President ever caught my eye.

The President opened things with a short heartfelt statement: "President Fox of Mexico is a man . . . a man from Mexico . . . Mexico is a country . . . a country that is . . . next to America." Despite his warm feelings for our neighbor to the south, the President made it clear that he opposed "amnesty blankets."

President Fox delivered a longer statement in Spanish. Then came the opening for questions.

Things got off to a rocky start when Jonathan Alter shouted a question about Mexico's opposition to the American invasion of Iraq. President Bush didn't seem to hear this. Gephardt the Albino did. He simply nodded and two sentries carried Alter away. The other reporters stood awkwardly, pretending not to notice. (Apparently this was protocol.) Then Laurie was recognized:

"Señor Presidente," she began with gravity. "Por favor, what do you think of Presidente Bush's perro, Barney?"

Scott and his press aides suddenly laughed easily—all except Gephardt, who never cracked a smile—as a wide warm grin spread over President Bush's face. He looked like a proud father.

President Fox turned to President Bush. "¿Quien es la bonita rubia con los labios suculentos?"

President Bush cheerfully answered in his charmingly clunky Spanish. "Es una reporter de Fox News."

President Fox instantly brightened. "Ay, claro. ¡Las chicas bonitas de Fox News son muy famosas!"

Laurie blushed but pressed for an answer to her question, ahora mismo. "¿Por favor, Señor Presidente, un answer to my question?"

President Fox was happy to oblige. "Entonces, el perro Barney es un perro muy inteligente y guapo." Once the interpreter had explained that President Fox thought Barney was intelligent and good-looking, there were laughs all around. Even the press corps applauded.

I was impressed by Laurie's ability to charm, but this was a rare opportunity to ask the President of the United States, in the presence of another world leader, an important question. I wasn't going to pass it up.

"EXCUSE ME!" I screamed as the President and his entourage had already begun filing out. There was a stunned silence. I shocked even myself with my volume, but it got their attention. Then without thinking, I blurted out my question: "What do you say to the hardworking immigrant who is often the scapegoat of disgruntled American workers?" I could have stopped there; the President actually looked like he was going to answer the question. But suddenly Helen's story, fanciful as it was, popped into my head and I couldn't stop myself: "I mean, Mr. President, are you going to do the right thing and honor Miss Pussy?"

President Bush's eyes widened suddenly. Scott and Gephardt the Albino shot me looks of death.

"Oh my God, you did NOT just say pussy," said Kate Snow incredulously.

"Easy, Mo, we're not in the army," said Jim Angle.

"¿Que es pussy?" asked President Fox.

There was no point in trying to explain myself. Scott addressed the press corps: "There will be no further questions. Mo, rest assured I will have words with Mr. Sorenson."

"Just remember, NBC has *nothing* to do with MSNBC," said Norah O'Donnell as everyone left.

Candy placed a hand on my shoulder. "Next time," she said, "try 'poon tang.' It might go over a little easier."

ERIC WAS SO ANGRY that I had to hold the phone away from my ear.

"How could you possibly use that kind of language? And in the Rose Garden of all places?" he shouted.

I was momentarily distracted by Howie Kurtz's *Washington Post* Media Notes column and his reference to my gaffe: "Rocca's Big Meow Mix-up."

"Mo, I don't think you're hearing me," continued Eric.

"Sorry about that, Eric. I'm listening. Look, there's an explanation."

After a pause, Eric gave me an opening. "I find that impossible to believe, but please explain."

"Well, in case you didn't know, Rutherford B. Hayes had a cat," I began, "the very first Siamese cat in America. Her name was Miss Pussy. And just as Chinese immigrants were being scapegoated during the 1870s economic slowdown, she contracted some sort of fatal bronchial infection and died. It was a very heartbreaking scene." I started petering out here. "So if you think about it, Eric, there was actually a very clear connection to the whole Mexican immigration issue."

I must have sounded touched because Eric suddenly became very gentle with me.

"Okay, Mo, we're going to slow things down a little for you. I know you've been under pressure so I'm not going to let you go just for this. Now I promised the White House that you wouldn't make a habit of this kind of behavior."

"But Eric—"

Eric's voice regained a little of its edge. "Three strikes and you're out seems fair. You're 1–0 right now."

We said our good-byes, then I headed out the door. I had a score to settle.

14

Helen Thomas
Underneath It All

"I'm sorry you didn't get to see me make a gigantic ass of myself," I snarled. I was standing in Helen's lair, steamed at her for having filled my head with such nonsense.

"Don't worry about Howie," she sighed. "Jeez, you'd think he could come up with a better pun than 'Meow Mix-up.' He's much better on TV."

"Excuse me, Helen, but I set out to deliver headlines from the White House, not make them."

"Darling, I think you're overreacting."

"Dammit, Helen, don't tell me I'm overreacting. I trusted you to guide me." Then I crossed the line. "Why I ever listened to that stupid children's story of yours I'll never know." I instantly felt badly. "I'm sorry, Helen, that was a terrible thing to say."

"Oh, honey, don't you think I can take criticism? I'll tell you one thing, the *New York Tribune* was a lot harsher."

The *New York Tribune* was abolitionist Horace Greeley's paper. It disappeared over eighty years ago, merging with the *New York Herald*.

"The *New York Tribune?*"

"That's right. They said my book didn't hold a candle to Jenny

Lind's children's book. Even back then it was all about celebrity children's books. To think they gave a rave to a book about an opera-singing duck with laryngitis. So the duck had to miss a couple of performances. Big whoop."

I was tired of ignoring the strange clues Helen kept dropping. Unless she was demented—and that was a distinct possibility— she had something to tell me.

"Helen," I said, "I need you to tell me the truth. When did you write that story about Miss Pussy?"

She looked me right in the eyes. "You don't want to know. You know why? Because it would destroy you!"

"That's not true!" I said.

"All right," she shrugged. "Then I'll tell you."

She took a few steps back and brought her hands up to the top button on her blouse. Suddenly she looked so vulnerable. I thought of the scene in *Yentl* when Barbra Streisand reveals to Mandy Patinkin that she is in fact a woman. (I wondered for a moment how Helen would sound on "Papa, Can You Hear Me?" It required a wider range than "Getting to Know You." I wondered also why Mandy Patinkin was cast in a movie musical and never allowed to sing in it.)

But Helen's revelation was far more shocking. As she opened her blouse—and I was preparing my It's-not-you-it's-me-but-I'm-really-very-flattered speech—I saw not flesh but what looked like a coat of feathers.

"Oh no, oh my God, Helen"—I was breathless—"are you . . . are you . . . ?"

"Yes, Mo," she said, her eyes moistening with tears. "I am. I'm a turkey buzzard."

15

Bird of a Nation

The turkey buzzard. *Cathartes aura*. I knew from my passing familiarity with nonpresidential animals that the turkey buzzard is the cousin of the California condor. The remarkable thing about the turkey buzzard (known to some as a turkey vulture) is its great lifespan. Some were known to live as many as 118 years. It has an extraordinary sense of smell. Contrary to popular belief, it has no relationship to a turkey. It simply has a similar-looking neck and red head, both destitute of feathers and sparsely covered with short black hair. (Helen apparently was blessed with more hair than normal on her head. As for her crop, it was barely visible. She might have had some work done.)

The turkey buzzard is found throughout most of the United States, mostly in the South and in maritime regions, but never farther east or north of New Jersey. It is a social animal and feeds on all sorts of food, with a preference for sucking the eggs and devouring the young of other birds, especially herons. It also eats other turkey buzzards, but only if they are already dead.

Its plumage is blackish brown, its tail purplish, its eyes brown. Although it is known for a startling appearance up close, with badly diseased skin around its eyes (here once again Helen was apparently blessed by good genes), it is equally renowned by a beauty in flight matched by few other birds, with a glorious wingspan of, on average, six feet four inches.

Beyond that I knew very little.

"I must confess, Helen, I don't know what to say."

By now she had taken off her skirt and shaken out her tail of twelve broad straight feathers.

"Excuse me, dear. It's awfully uncomfortable keeping all that

Portrait of a young Helen.

crammed inside a girdle. Now let's have that talk: As you might have guessed, I'm older than you think."

"Well, exactly how—?"

"Mind your manners. I might be a different species, but I'm still a female. Some turkey buzzards live to be around 120. Let's just say I'm older than the average.

"My story really begins in August 1805. I was very young—you could have counted the number of times I'd molted on one claw at that point. I lived with the Shoshone Indians in an area called the Lehmi Pass, just along the Idaho-Montana border. Imagine Ruby Ridge, but less commercial. The Indians called the cliff I perched on Solemn Heath."

"The Lehmi Pass. That's where Lewis and Clark trekked, looking for the headwaters of the Columbia River," I said, stating the obvious.

"Well, they never would have found them, if not for their Indian guide Sacagawea. Sacagawea led those two boys and their corps of discovery to our camp in search of horses. That was the only way they'd be able to cross the Rockies before they'd catch their death of cold. Someone really should have told them to pack warmer clothes."

"They got their horses, right?"

"And they got me. Truth is, I was bored hanging out all day on a perch. It's no place for a young buzzard with ambition. So I followed Sac. And let me tell you, she was an inspiration. She wasn't only guiding the expedition. She had to deal with a baby, a whiny French husband, *and* Meriwether Lewis. Lewis was a nice young man, but he could be very gloomy."

"Well, yes," I broke in, "he ended up killing himself. So, Helen, I bet you were a big help."

"Mainly I helped keep everyone on track along the treacherous Lolo Trail. Those were the roughest eleven days of my life, aside from my trip to China with Nixon. Bad moo shoo," she explained.

"But I thought turkey buzzards can eat anything," I said.

"I hope you haven't been reading that Audubon crap," she snapped. "Let me tell you something. Ornithologists don't know jack. They're the used-car salesmen of animal scientists. Got it?"

"Uh, sure."

"But I digress. We all spent the winter of 1805–6 on the Oregon coast. It was horrible. Constant raining, constant flooding. I haven't been back to the beach since. But being with Sacagawea made it all worth it. Lewis and Clark might have had greatness in them, but they couldn't have done it without the guidance of Sacagawea."

"Wait a sec, Helen, I get that you're a turkey buzzard. In retrospect it seems obvious. But why has everyone all these years thought that you're Lebanese?"

"I haven't a clue. It might be because I've always liked chickpeas—that winter, Sacagawea and I used to mash them up and spread it on bread. We couldn't afford yeast since we'd spent all our wampum on horses, so the bread was unleavened."

"You were making hummus and pita bread?"

"Is that what the kids are calling it? All I know is that when my colleagues saw me eating it in the pressroom, they started calling me Lebanese. It only became awkward once, in 1992, when Jamie Farr attended the White House Correspondents Dinner."

"Okay, so back to the story. How did you get to Washington?"

"Well, Lewis and Clark sent a couple of grizzly bears back to Washington, D.C. I had nothing else to do, so I hitched a ride. Never share a buggy with two grizzlies," she said with a knowing glance.

"Washington was just a big old swamp back then," she continued, "trash festering in open landfills. It was delicious! Of course, Jefferson was President, which was a delight. He was so intellectually curious. You know about Dick the mockingbird."

I knew that after Buzzy the sheepdog, Dick was Jefferson's

favorite pet. He would perch on the President's shoulder and sing along as Jefferson played his violin. So what?

"Such a nice Jewish bird," Helen said. "Of course Jefferson didn't know that until he found Dick's yarmulke hidden in the Monticello dumbwaiter. Then the two became the best of friends. Jefferson wrote the Virginia Statute for Religious Freedom in honor of him. And Dick got the President hooked on klezmer."

"Jefferson played klezmer on his *violin*?" I asked.

"You want that I should tell you the story? Stop interrupting. Oy."

Then Helen started sounding more cautious. "You know, back then pets were treated . . . differently . . . with more respect. Being an animal myself, and one with a real interest in politics, I was naturally interested in, well, presidential pets."

Naturally, I thought. The fact that a turkey buzzard was talking to me made everything she actually said seem all the less weird.

She continued carefully. "So I started researching, gathering articles and artifacts, doing some writing"—she gestured with her wing toward her cabinet and bookcases—"documenting the presidential pets. But eventually it became, well, unacceptable for a turkey buzzard to ask questions. So I went underground, so to speak. Then in 1943 I reemerged as Helen Thomas. And since the Kennedy administration I've covered the White House."

My head was spinning. "So since 1806 you've lived in D.C.? You never went back home, even for a visit?"

"No, dear. And I still think about Solemn Heath every day."

It suddenly occurred to me: "Solemn Heath! That's an anagram for 'Helen Thomas'!"

"You're good."

Then impulsively I asked, "Helen, I have to ask, in all the time you've been here, have you ever been a presidential pet yourself?"

"NO!!" she shot back. The question jarred her, but she quickly reined it in. "No, dear. What on earth would ever make you think that? I've always been an . . . observer."

"I'm sorry to ask such a personal question, Helen. It's just that your story is so amazing. You've got to write it down. You could get a killer advance."

She looked at me intently. "No, Mo. My story can never be told. In fact no one can know the truth about me. It could endanger all of this." Again she indicated her archives. "You must keep this secret and anything else I tell you, at least for now. Right now just listen and learn. This story is big—bigger than a single President and his dog, cat, bobcat, or giraffe."

"Giraffe?! Who had a giraffe?"

"Chet Arthur. It was just an overnight guest. He was a strange guy. But that's not my point. My point is, you must be careful."

Helen looked so scared. In such a short time we'd come so far. I instinctively reached out and grabbed her claw.

"Of course Helen, your secret is safe with me."

She glanced down. "You know, Mo, I've been through a lot. It's not just the way the press office has treated me or even the other members of the press corps." Her beak was trembling now.

"What is it, Helen?"

"Please, don't speak. Right now I just need you to stay with me."

16

The Age of Jackass

The next morning I awoke in Helen's bed. If Marlin Perkins and Jacqueline Susann had collaborated on a novel, I was living it. Stranger still, this was all happening without the popping of any pills. (Prevacid doesn't count.)

The mattress was actually a futon, one of the only pieces of furniture from the twentieth century, and it was surprisingly comfortable. Helen had picked it up from Mike Deaver's yard sale in 1985.

Helen had already gone. I sat up, wiped the sleep from my eyes, spat out some feathers, and looked for my glasses. I was nearly blind without them, so I wasn't sure what was causing the rustling sound that came from high up in Helen's bookshelves. I looked over and saw a short whitish figure atop a ladder busily filing away volumes. It looked like the great historian Arthur Schlesinger—if he had floppy ears.

"Excuse me, but who are you?" I said, clearing my throat and fumbling for my specs.

"Well, hello, my boy," he said matter-of-factly, in a slightly British accent. "Your spectacles are on Madame's nightstand."

They were there, right next to a jar of paraffin emulsion, which

Helen used to waterproof her feathers. (Helen specially ordered this beauty product from Crayola.) Once I got my glasses on, I could focus on the gentleman in the stacks.

Or should I say gentle *dog*? It was the beagle who'd spoken cryptically to me at Laurie's book party, from inside the kennel. But now he was wearing a red bow tie and round, dark-rimmed glasses. He looked exactly like the character Mr. Peabody from my favorite Rocky and Bullwinkle cartoon spin-off, *Peabody's Improbable History*.

In fact it *was* Mr. Peabody!

"MY GOD, YOU'RE Mr. Peabody. What are you doing here?"

"It's really quite simple. I work for Madame," he said, descending from the ladder. "I've been her loyal assistant and archivist for a long time. I overheard everything last night . . . unfortunately," he added drolly. "Now that you and she have become so familiar, shall we say, I suppose I can be more forthcoming."

As cartoon fans everywhere knew, Mr. Peabody used to educate Sherman, the bespectacled boy he'd adopted, with trips in his WABAC time machine. Had he taken Helen for a ride in it?

"No, Mo, I no longer try to meddle with history. I'm now devoted to aiding Madame in her quest to recall history as it really was and preserve it for the future. Those who cannot remember the past—"

I wasn't interested in discussing Santayana. I had more pressing concerns. "Right, right, Mr. Peabody. So whatever happened to Sherman? You two were such a great team."

"Well, after I took the boy back in time for a visit with Professor Leo Strauss at the University of Chicago, Sherman fell under the spell of the nascent neocon movement. I lost contact with him soon after. Today he can be seen on George Stephanopolous's struggling Sunday morning program."

Mr. Peabody

"Sherman is George Will?!"

"Yes, that is his nom de punditry, I've been told."

Mr. Peabody continued. "In any event, I grew tired of time travel. It struck me as entirely too gimmicky. Then I heard about the work that Madame was doing."

Mr. Peabody's was a voice I implicitly trusted. While some questions had been answered the night before, I was still hazy on the mystery of Helen's fixation with all the Presidents' pets. Could she possibly believe that *any* President had had a significant relationship with a pet? Maybe Helen was just a little too long in the gobbler.

"So much has been thrown at me so quickly," I said. "I want to understand."

Mr. Peabody filed away a biography of William Henry Harrison's cow Sukey, then grabbed a tray of scones and began serving me breakfast as he started in on his lecture.

"Harry Truman, our thirty-third President, once said, 'If you want a friend in Washington, get a dog.' The old haberdasher was known for being blunt. There is no greater example of his bluntness than that statement. A true friend tells you what you need to know—supports you, yes, but helps keep you on the right path in life when you begin to stray. This is what pets have done for almost all of our Presidents. Coffee?"

"Please. Well, all the Presidents have had pets," I said. "All except Millard Fillmore."

At the mention of Millard Fillmore, Mr. Peabody flashed a startled look at me, then regained his train of thought and continued pouring. "The pets, in short, have humanized our Chief Executives when they ran the risk of losing touch with the people they serve. No leader, after all, can possibly serve his people without sensible counsel. And the human advisors are all too often dehumanizing forces."

I wasn't much for New Ageism, but as a former Manhattanite I was certainly used to friends who treated their pets like children. Doggie birthday parties, dog mitzvahs even, had become de rigueur in some circles. This was no weirder.

"Fair enough," I said, taking a sip and noticing that I was being served on official Franklin Pierce White House china, one of my favorite among the rococo-revival presidential patterns. "I can see how a pet can make a person gentler. Thank you." Mr. Peabody had just finished slicing a honeydew melon for me. "Pets lower blood pressure," I continued. "And if they're really adorable they can make you giggle—"

Mr. Peabody cut me off and looked grave. "It's more than that, my boy. From the founding of the republic White House pets have lent vital perspective. They've helped define the nature of the presidency itself," he added dramatically.

"Okay, you're getting a little out there," I said.

"Oh ye of little faith. Let's start at the very beginning then. Frittata?"

"If it's not too much trouble. Can you make it with egg whites only?"

"Of course."

Mr. Peabody, apparently an expert multitasker, began scrambling and explaining. "George Washington and the presidency. You remember that Washington was more god than man when he arrived at the Constitutional Convention in Philadelphia in May of 1787. The executive office was undefined and in danger of becoming kinglike."

"That's true," I concurred. "The very next month Alexander Hamilton gave a speech at the convention proposing that the President be chosen for life."

"Right you are, my boy," confirmed Mr. Peabody. "Then you likely know that John Adams wanted Washington to be referred to as 'His Majesty, the President.' Even worse he went on record singing the praises of hereditary succession."

"Yes," I said, "but Washington was never going to go for any of that. He modeled himself after the great Cincinnatus," I said, referring of course to the fifth-century BC warrior who rescued Rome, then returned to his simple farm life when the job was finished. "Even though Washington could have assumed dictatorial power he rejected it at every turn. Just like Cincinnatus, he walked away from it."

"If you were a dog, I would throw you a bone . . . IF you had answered completely. The truth is, Washington was influenced by something much more immediate, namely the goings-on at his beloved estate, Mount Vernon. Careful, the plate's hot."

"Thank you, it looks delicious. What does Mount Vernon have to do with this?"

"It was at Mount Vernon," continued Mr. Peabody, "that General Washington, in his quest to create a line of 'super mules,' imported a blue-blooded donkey to mate with his mares. The donkey, named Royal Gift, was a present from the King of Spain. And this Andalusian ass occupied a stable right next to General W's trusty steed Nelson."

"Nelson was Washington's beloved horse throughout the Revolutionary War," I said. "He was even with him at Valley Forge."

"A heroic horse, indeed," said Mr. Peabody, "and a striking contrast with Royal Gift." With that he handed me a written log signed by none other than George Washington.

17

First in War, First in Peace, First in the Field of Animal Husbandry

The chart was a day-to-day comparison of the behavior of Nelson versus the behavior of Royal Gift.

Nelson the horse	*Royal Gift the donkey*
Day 1 — Up early. Plowed fields.	Up late. Brayed loudly.
Day 2 — Up earlier. Plowed fields. Mild scurvy. Did not complain.	Up later. Brayed more loudly.
Day 3 — Up early. Plowed fields. Shared barley with indigent sheep. Plowed fields some more.	Swilled ale. Mounted mare in three minutes. Vomited on her.
Day 4 — Allowed young slave girls to brush mane and ride sidesaddle.	Stole ham. Kicked slave.

Day 5	Saved old woman from drowning in river. Refused reward of extra barley.	Stared at self in mirror all day long, ignoring cries of old woman drowning nearby. Mounted new mare. Did not return calls from first mare.
Day 6	Recovered stolen buckwheat from herd of rabid Hessian oxen. Sustained grievous ox-horn wounds. Returned home and plowed fields.	Stayed up all night gossiping and belittling pigs and other livestock, depriving them of rest. Slept all day. Woke up and mounted third mare.
Day 7	Drew up will bequeathing hooves for gelatin for poor children.	Killed a baby partridge, "just to watch it die."

"The corrupting influence of royalism was never writ clearer," said Mr. Peabody. "The behavioral profiles of these animals confirmed Washington's deepest-held suspicions of the dissolute nature of monarchy. Especially at the end of his service, when he was tempted to retain the power and trappings that were offered to him as President, he pondered the noble example of Nelson."

I couldn't help but think of Washington's Farewell Address. "So when Washington warned us about the danger of foreign entanglements he was thinking of—"

"Royal Gift, my boy, and those poor mares, not to mention the female donkeys, also known as jennets. In fact Mount Vernon opened the nation's very first jennet crisis center, that's how bad the damage was. 'Take back the night,' I can still hear them braying. Please don't get up," Mr. Peabody said as he cleared my plates for me.

As impressed as I was by the document, I wasn't convinced of anything extraordinary. "Okay, so maybe Washington was influenced by his pets. That's no stranger than a few First Ladies talking to the dead," I said, thinking of Mary Todd Lincoln, Florence Harding, Nancy Reagan, and Hillary Clinton.

But Mr. Peabody wasn't letting me off that easy. "It is hardly so random, Mo. The truth is far deeper than you realize. Moments ago, you recounted to me the decision by Cincinnatus to resist absolute power."

"That's right," I said. "He walked away from it."

"There's the rub, my boy. He didn't 'walk' away from anything. He was on horseback when he crossed the Tiber to return to his farm—but he was carried against his will. Cincinnatus, I'm afraid, had begun lusting for power. But his horse Sadie—that's the modern translation of her name—refused to take him anywhere but back to the farm. In the end he simply relented to her better judgment."

Mr. Peabody took his time towel-drying the plates—with its ornate caryatids, the punchbowl required special care—and turned around to deliver his thesis.

"Thus was born a compact between animals and human leaders. A compact bound by the indispensable 'Sacred Animal' component of proper decision-making."

" 'Sacred Animal'?" I said, rising to my feet. "Mr. Peabody, that's an anagram for 'A Salad Mincer'!" Those were the very first words he'd spoken from the kennel at Laurie's book party.

"It's about time," he huffed. "Now it must be acknowledged that the compact has not always been observed as it should be. Caligula was an especially incorrigible human. The *only* intelligent thing he did was appoint his horse to the Senate."

I couldn't resist. "So I guess Caligula had good horse sense?" Mr. Peabody stared at me blankly.

"Okay, Mr. Peabody," I continued after an awkward silence. "You're claiming that this 'compact' connects Cincinnatus and Sadie, with Washington and Nelson, with Hayes and Miss Pussy?"

"Indeed it does," he replied. "And the essence of this compact between President and pet was very clearly promulgated at the founding of this nation. You're familiar with John Jay, I assume."

"He was the first Chief Justice of the Supreme Court and the author of five of the Federalist Papers," I answered. While Hamilton and Madison had apparently competed over whose contribution was greater, it was easy to forget that there was a third writer. I'd always wondered why Jay was only able to turn out five against Hamilton's fifty-two and Madison's twenty-eight. Writer's block?

"Someone needs to do some fact checking," Mr. Peabody admonished me. "John Jay wrote *one hundred and six* of the most exciting and persuasive papers in support of the Constitution and the role of the executive, in particular. This way, please."

Mr. Peabody led me over to the periodicals section of the archives and pulled out an edition of the *Independent Journal,* one of the two papers which originally carried the Federalist Papers. This edition included "Federalist No. 173: The Mitigating Role of The Presidential Pet against Tyrannical Rule in the Executive." It read in part:

Men of factious tempers or sinister designs or suspect capacity may, upon obtaining suffrages, betray the interests of the people. While Republics may best favor the election of a proper guardian of the common weal, the final safeguard is the counsel and advocacy of an animal of the non-human species. In other words, our system is good, but not foolproof. A blockhead could very well get elected president and

if he's surrounded by madmen and unchecked by Congress or the judiciary or the press, we're all screwed. So make sure he listens to his pet.
PUBLIUS

"By many estimations, this is the particular article that tipped the scales in favor of ratification," said Mr. Peabody. "People felt more comfortable with the assurance that a pet would be on hand."

"If it's true, it's pretty sensational," I admitted. "What happened to John Jay's other Federalist Papers?"

"Most of the others were about pet care. They're fairly outdated now. I mean really, does anyone still recommend the use of leeches on a gassy cat?" Mr. Peabody asked. "Sadly they've all been expurgated from the modern editions of the Federalist Papers, though I do have most of them on microfiche."

If this was all one big lie, it was a doozie for sure, and brilliant. For the moment I chose to give him the benefit of my many doubts. "All right, Mr. Peabody, I can *maybe* understand the need for a special kind of advisor at the beginning of the republic to represent the wishes of the people. Few Americans were allowed to vote after all. But once we became more of a democracy, the people were more directly in charge and—"

"—and the role of the presidential pet simply evolved. It became no less important. During Andrew Jackson's term, Alexis de Tocqueville was impressed enough that he—"

"—wrote about Jackson's foul-mouthed parrot Pol?" I guessed. Pol was infamous in his day, especially after cursing throughout Old Hickory's funeral.

"You catch on quickly. 'Old Hickory' was our first president to represent the 'common man.' And who better to speak for the American people than a common gutter-mouthed parrot? *S'il vous plaît,*" he said as he pulled volume 3 of de Tocqueville's *Democracy in America* and tossed it to me. It was so heavy that I nearly fell backward. I opened it up to the bookmarked passage.

"The Peculiar Mouthpiece of the Common Individual in American Democracy" read in part:

I confess that in America I saw more than America; I sought there the image of democracy itself, with its unbridled character, its prejudices, and its passions. What I found was President Jackson's parrot Pol issuing pronouncements like:

Veto the National Bank, dammit!
Oppose the South Carolina Ordinance of Nullification, dammit!
Our Federal Union: It must be preserved, dammit!
Suffrage for all white men, dammit!
Spoils system, dammit!
Recognize the Republic of Texas, dammit!
I like cheese, dammit!

Mr. Peabody replaced the volume. "Suffice it to say, Pol did *not* suggest the eviction and murder of the Creek Indians. Though his apparent enthusiasm for the spoils system is a bit troubling."

18

A Conspiracy So Great

The learning curve was very steep but I prided myself on being a quick study. "All right, Mr. Peabody, I can accept that pets played this role way back when. So what happened?"

"Two words: Theodore Roosevelt," Mr. Peabody intoned. "A man of unquestionable genius, but also a man who wanted to, in modern parlance, 'supersize' the presidency and consolidate his power. He knew that with the advent of sound and motion-picture technology, the President would be seen and heard by Americans on a mass scale. And he wanted to control and enhance his image. So he did something brilliant.

"He gave the correspondents covering him a pressroom in the White House," Mr. Peabody continued. "The reporters were now organized *under his* roof. They would now get their stories in a more orderly, controlled way. Controlled, of course, by the White House. And the story they would consistently get and disseminate was one of an increasingly superheroic Chief Executive. In the case of President Roosevelt, the White House's strategy was an immediate success. The reporters became his de facto publicists."

As a longtime fan of TR and a member of the Theodore

Roosevelt Association, I was naturally sensitive to any suggestion that he was less than superhuman. "Mr. Peabody, are you denying that President Roosevelt really did all those great things? What about the Panama Canal, the trust busting, conservation?"

"Now, now, my boy. All of those things indeed happened. But what you of all people should know is that Mr. Roosevelt had thirty-six pets, more than any other President."

"That's right, and Coolidge is right behind with thirty-three."

"I think you mean thirty-two," he said coolly.

"No, Mr. Peabody. I think I mean *thirty-three.*"

"Don't sass talk me when you know very well that Coolidge's mynah bird was a *vice*-presidential pet!"

I stood corrected.

"Now, as I was saying," he continued, "Theodore Roosevelt had the most presidential pets. And with that many pets, TR, a man even his most ardent partisans would describe as egomaniacal, felt particularly vulnerable to charges that he relied on the counsel of others. But rely on them he did."

Mr. Peabody sat me down on Helen's ottoman and began grilling me rapid-fire: "Quickly now, who convinced him to double the number of national parks?"

"Um, Algonquin the pony?"

"Who convinced him to support striking mine workers?"

"I don't know, Josiah the badger?"

"What about the Panama Canal?"

"Maybe Baron Spreckle the hen?"

"The Sherman Antitrust Act?"

"Slippers the six-toed cat?"

"The Pure Food and Drug Act?"

"Father O'Grady the guinea pig?"

"The Roosevelt Corollary to the Monroe Doctrine?"

"Uh . . . gee, I . . ."

"I can't HEAR you!"

"Jonathan the piebald rat?"

Mr. Peabody was all up in my face screaming.

"RESOLVE THE RUSSO-JAPANESE CONFLICT?!"

I started cracking. "Oh gosh, um, the zebra? I—I don't know his name."

"I'M WAITING!"

"Uh . . . Xander? Claude? Phyllis? I—I—I—"

"DO YOU WANT ANSWERS?!"

"I—I—I—"

"DO YOU WANT THE TRUTH?!!"

". . . Ned?"

"YOU CAN'T HANDLE THE TRUTH!!!"

I snapped. "JUST STOP IT, MR. PEABODY! I don't know the zebra's name. Okay?" I broke down sobbing. "You happy now?"

Mr. Peabody sat down next to me and gently patted my head. "There, there, my boy. The zebra had no name. I was just testing you. You have to be strong to handle the kind of information I'm giving you."

He handed me a tissue. I wiped the tears from my eyes and pulled myself together. "Okay, I'm back now. So Teddy Roosevelt's White House began taking control of the press so it could tell its own story—with him as the one and only star."

"I couldn't have put it more succinctly," he said. "Not long after TR's tenure—in February of 1914, to be precise—the reporters created the White House Correspondents Association. The White House, now under the nominal control of President Woodrow Wilson, was just fine with this. Now the members of the press corps could be tracked all the more easily."

"Wilson certainly benefited from a tight rein on the press," I said, blowing my nose. "After his stroke in 1919, his wife practically ran the White House."

"They called her the First Woman President or the Presidentress," Mr. Peabody said. "But by now you should realize that 'they' got it wrong. Edith was shielding her husband from the

While Baron Spreckle the hen advised President Roosevelt on the incitement of Panamanian rebels and the terms of the Hay-Bunau-Varilla Treaty, Eli Yale the macaw, seen here with Theodore Jr., actually surveyed the route of the Panama Canal by air.

press because he was holed up with his ram, Old Ike, desperately trying to salvage his bid to join the League of Nations."

Mr. Peabody handed me a picture of an ailing Wilson with Old Ike curled up at the foot of the bed with a steno pad.

"That's just wrong," I said uneasily.

"What do you expect? He was a university professor. They're the kinkiest."

"Good point."

"Of course, occasionally signs of the real influence of pets appeared." Mr. Peabody pulled back a curtain, revealing a copy of Mrs. Coolidge's official White House portrait in which she

First Lady Grace Coolidge and Rebecca the raccoon, before a rabid Rebecca savagely attacked presidential son John in the Vermeil Room. Rob Roy the collie came to the rescue.

appeared with her collie, Rob Roy. "Insiders knew that this was a gesture of thanks from the Coolidges after the dog rescued their young son John from a ferocious raccoon attack in the Vermeil Room."

"That sounds like the plotline from any old episode of *Lassie*."

"Well, where do you think the producers got the idea for the series?" asked Mr. Peabody.

"Wow," I said, then paused. "Am I getting any credit for this?"

"I'm afraid we don't do work-study at the presidential pet archives." Mr. Peabody continued with his lecture. "Finally the four-times-elected President Franklin Delano Roosevelt, a great man, but nonetheless one who liked power even more than his fifth cousin Teddy, appointed the first White House press secretary, Stephen Early, and the press came under even tighter control."

"Actually, Hoover's press secretary, George Akerson, was the first," I said haughtily, getting back at Mr. Peabody for making me cry earlier.

"I stand corrected," said Mr. Peabody. "Akerson is easy to forget, as is Hoover's elkhound Weejie. Both of them knew that their President was toast and spent most of their time packing his bags for the Waldorf.* Stephen Early was the first press secretary, I should say, to move aggressively to shield the inner workings of the President from the public."

"I guess that's true," I said. "In over twelve years in office, FDR was photographed only *once* in a wheelchair."

"And the tremendous contributions of Fala the Scottie were hidden from the public."

It was undeniable that Mr. Peabody had built a compelling case. Still one question kept gnawing at me. "Mr. Peabody, it's

---

* Hoover lived at New York's Waldorf Towers until his death in 1964.

not like modern presidential pets are hidden from the press. Millie, Socks, Buddy, and Barney—they all get overwhelming coverage."

"Coverage of a *different* kind. They're portrayed as cute play-things, so that the President can look even more imposing. It's terrific propaganda for the White House. But quite frankly it's insulting to any self-respecting four-legged presidential pet scholar." I assumed he meant himself. " 'Man's best friend' has become a cruel mockery of the role these pets were meant to play—and still play."

"Still play?"

"The tapes don't lie."

With that Mr. Peabody slid open a cabinet door, revealing a wall of recording equipment. He clicked PLAY on one of the recorders.

"He's gone off riding with Camilla again. I'm so terribly lonely in this dreary palace," said the halting voice of a vulnerable young British woman. "It seems my only friends are the Queen's corgis."

Mr. Peabody abruptly hit STOP. "Pardon me, that's the Diana, Princess of Wales, tape. I meant to play this." He grabbed a tape labeled August 4, 1964, inserted it, and hit PLAY.

19

The Dog of War

I instantly recognized the voice from C-SPAN Radio's Saturday-afternoon broadcasts. It was LBJ. Mr. Peabody helpfully handed me a written transcript with footnotes from historian Michael Beschloss.

JOHNSON: Him,[1] my friend, how are you doing?

HIM: Just fine, Mr. President. Just fine.

JOHNSON: And how's the little lady? You know I love Her.[2] The two of you need to come on over and let Lady Bird fix you some leftovers.

HIM: Thank you, Mr. President. Last weekend we snuck out to take a peek at Route 95, just south of the city. Mrs. Johnson has done a fine job beautifying that highway.

JOHNSON (LAUGHING): There you go sugaring me up. You're just about the smartest son of a bitch I ever met. I told you before, I'm sure glad to have you inside the doghouse pissing out, 'stead of outside pissing in.

---

1. Him was one of LBJ's two beagles.
2. Her was the other.

[momentarily distracted] Bob, get me a fresh roll, will you?[3]

HIM: Well, thank you, Mr. President.

JOHNSON: Now, Him, you're about as wise as a tree full of owls and as busy as a man with one hoe and two rattlesnakes—you don't mind all these animal expressions, do you?

HIM: Not at all, Mr. President.

JOHNSON: Good. Then you won't mind my saying that being President is like being a jackass in a hailstorm. There's nothing to do but stand there and take it. But this time I can't just stand there. A couple days back the destroyer USS *Maddox* got into a little back-'n-forth with some of the North Vietnamese in the Gulf of Tonkin. One attack I can handle. But then earlier today one of our sonar men thinks he just may have detected a *second* attack. Now there are no actual reports of an attack, visibility is seriously limited, and sonar is extremely unreliable, but I really don't want to look like a wuss next to Goldwater.[4] [to McNamara] Thanks, Bob. Now why don't you ever say hello to Jumbo.[5]

HIM: Well, Mr. President, I must be truthful. I'd caution you against using today's suspicious sonar report as an excuse to escalate what could very well become a quagmire in Southeast Asia. Why not just wait to act until we're sure we have our facts straight? I'd hate to see all that you want to accomplish in health, education, and civil rights eclipsed by thirty thousand body bags coming back on your clock—all because of what one man *thinks* he heard. Even my ears deceive me once in a while—and I've got ears more—

JOHNSON: Did you say something, Him? Louder than a cat pissing on a flat rock in here.[6]

---

3. The President is seated in the bathroom. Defense Secretary McNamara is close at hand.
4. Barry Goldwater was the Republican nominee for the upcoming election.
5. Jumbo was President Johnson's name for his Johnson. Oh my.
6. The President is relieving himself in the sink. Oh dear.

HIM: I was just saying, Mr. President, that—

JOHNSON: Couldn't agree more, Him. I'm going on TV tonight to announce a strike on North Vietnamese bases. We'll take out their petroleum reserves before sunrise. Looks like we've got a real Gulf of Tonkin incident on our hands.

HIM: Actually, Mr. President—

JOHNSON: Don't you worry, I'll go to Congress for a war resolution pronto—give them the old Johnson Treatment—though I gotta say that a joint committee's as useless as tits on a bull.[7] [background laughter] Valenti loves that one.

HIM: Mr. President, that's not—

JOHNSON: Thanks for your support, little feller. You're the best.

Mr. Peabody stopped the tape.

"Of course Johnson got his resolution and a terrible war with it," said Mr. Peabody. "Him had been right to be skeptical. Johnson himself admitted later that our navy was probably 'shooting at whales out there.' When things went bad and Him said 'I told you so,' the President took it out on Him."

Mr. Peabody showed me the infamous picture of Johnson lifting Him by the ears.

"I know that picture," I said. "Johnson said that he was just playing."

"Hardly. His ego was too big and too fragile to withstand any criticism. On the other hand, when things went well, the 'Johnson treatment' was quite different."

Mr. Peabody then handed me a picture with LBJ and his later dog, Yuki. "Here they are, celebrating passage of the Voting Rights Act of 1965."

---

7. Some bulls do in fact have tits. Oh, that's pretty hot.

LBJ, angry over Vietnam, takes it out on adviser Him the beagle.

The tape and supporting pictures lent irrefutable support to Helen's and Mr. Peabody's assertions. Pets were still actively advising Presidents, or at least trying to. But with each question answered, another took its place: "Why would today's press ignore all this?" I asked. "It's such an amazing story, with such major consequences for our country."

"The answer is quite simple, my boy," said Mr. Peabody. "Most don't know about the role pets once played. The White House, in the clearest sign yet of its contempt for the fourth estate, has

LBJ celebrating passage of the Voting Rights Act with Yuki the mutt.

successfully erased almost all evidence present and past. What remains is here." He gestured to Helen's archives.

"So the other members of the press don't even know . . . ?" I asked.

"Most of them don't. And that of course is a bad thing for the public. The press are the guardians, the watchdogs, of the public interest. When the White House achieves total isolation, it becomes dangerous—for the people . . . and the pets."

"Dangerous?! Mr. Peabody, let's cut to the chase here. Is Barney in any sort of danger?"

Mr. Peabody turned and faced me directly, clearly laying it on the line.

"Let me be very clear, Mo: The President genuinely loves having a ball of fur to roll around with and baby-talk to in an unnervingly childlike fashion." Mr. Peabody slid open a different cabinet door, revealing a plasma screen playing the President's latest Barney holiday video. In it the President was pretending to sleep when Andrew Card, dressed as Santa Claus, tiptoed in with a gift-wrapped Barney. President Bush "woke up" and opened the package, surprised and overjoyed by his gift. Barney looked miserable as the President jumped up and down on the bed cradling him.

Mr. Peabody continued. "These images suit the press office just fine. They make the President 'likable.' But mark my word: If Barney tries to influence the President in any substantial way—if he tries to be anything more than the public relations tool that they want—then the inner circle will turn on him."

A final thought on this subject occurred to me. "Mr. Peabody, the press at large may not know anything about any of this. But at least Laurie Dhue would know, wouldn't she? She has complete access."

Mr. Peabody raised one eyebrow. "A fine question, Mo. A very fine question. Now, if you don't mind, I've got some paperwork to take care of." And Mr. Peabody receded into the archive stacks.

20

Book Clubbed

The next day I awoke—in my own apartment—with a renewed sense of purpose. I would no longer dance around my beat, searching for clever ways to ask about other topics.

Today members of the press corps were covering an event that was part of Laura Bush's annual National Book Festival. These events had made news, because of both the diversity of writers—many of them fiercely outspoken opponents of the President—and the unanimity of praise among these authors for Mrs. Bush. She won over virtually everyone she met.

As luck should have it the topic of that day's gathering was animal literature. Among today's guest authors was former First Lady Barbara Bush, author of *Millie's Book,* the "autobiography" of the elder President Bush's springer spaniel and a gigantic best-seller. The late Millie was mother to the current President Bush's first First Dog, Spot—himself only recently deceased. (Some speculated that he'd choked on a dog biscuit.)

The elder Mrs. Bush remained one of the modern White House's great characters. An event with both Mrs. Bushes was not to be missed. Helen was feeling under the weather so she would not be attending.

The rest of us were ushered into the East Room for the opening of the day's event by the First Lady's press secretary, the boyishly good-looking Gordon Johndroe. Gordon was far less guarded than Scott. With the chipper energy of a student council president, he reflected the First Lady's open, easy air perfectly.

The honored guests were seated in a semicircle. Laura Bush rose to meet us and put us all at ease with a gentle "Good to see you all," her soft twang unfailingly charming. She wore a modest blue suit and a big Texas smile. Before returning to her seat, she gave Candy a little squeeze on the arm. "I'm thinkin' about you, darlin'," she said in a hush.

"Thank you, Mrs. Bush," said Candy, sniffling. It occurred to me only then that today was the anniversary of the violent rodeo death of Candy's lover Chet. With all that Mrs. Bush had going on, it impressed me that she could remember such a personal detail.

Laura Bush took her seat at one end of the semicircle. Filling out the other seats were *Cujo* author Stephen King and Amy Tan, who brought along her dog Mr. Zo, subject of her next book. Marxist lesbian poet activist Gambia Baraka, sister of the radical New Jersey poet laureate Amiri Baraka, sat at the end opposite Laura Bush. Despite her politics, Gambia's recently published retelling of Ashanti animal folktales had captivated Mrs. Bush.

Finally, Barbara Bush sat in the center on what could only be described as a throne. She was impeccably put together, her Greenwich Granite exterior worn not one bit since the days before the Clinton interregnum. She heartily lobbed one at an old pal: "Don't think you can hide from me, Angle," she called out to Fox News's Jim Angle. "I'm not blind yet."

Jim blushed. "Good to see you, Mrs. Bush."

"All right, that's enough. Where's the real star?" she snapped. Who else could she have meant? Laurie, dressed in an elegant elephant-print suit—in honor of the Republican royalty—spoke up.

"Good morning, Mrs. Bush. It's so good to have you back at the White House. Of course it's not like you really ever left."

Barbara Bush chortled. "George and I like to call those eight years our 'hiatus.' " The press corps laughed as she took a swig of her iced tea. "And might I add, Laurie, that lipstick looks sensational."

Once the din quieted, Laura Bush rose again to address us. "Welcome all to this very special gathering of some of my favorite authors. Like pieces of a vibrant mosaic, the books they have written add new color and form to an already existing body of great—"

"This room really is drafty, don't you think?" The elder Mrs. Bush was casually starting up a conversation with Stephen King. An embarrassed Laura Bush turned around and looked at her mother-in-law.

"Oh, I'm sorry, Laura dear," said Barbara Bush. "I didn't realize you'd started speaking."

Laura Bush, always deferential, simply nodded. "That's all right, Mother." She turned back around and continued. "It has been said that a good book is like an unreachable itch; you just can't leave it alone. That's certainly an analogy a household pet might understand."

The press corps laughed obligingly.

The elder Mrs. Bush again turned to Stephen King. "It surprises me, but sometimes she can be funny." King seemed as uncomfortable as were the rest of us with Barbara Bush's candid remarks. She then turned to Amy Tan and gestured to a table at the side of the room. "Now how on God's green earth did they get those tablecloths so white?"

"I don't know. Ancient Chinese secret?" an unamused Amy Tan answered drily.

Barbara Bush just shrugged, then stuck out her right hand. "So what do you think of my nails?"

The dead silence that followed was broken once again by the demure Laura Bush.

"Well then, let's have some questions." The younger Mrs. Bush didn't play favorites. She called on Kate Snow first. "Yes, Kate."

"Mrs. Bush, how important is reading?"

"Call in the think tank," barked Barbara Bush sarcastically. "We'll be up all night on this one."

Perhaps it wasn't the toughest question, but Laura Bush gently answered it: "Kate, it's very important for all of us as individuals and as a community to read. You know, I have always believed that the importance of a book lies in its power to turn a solitary act into a shared vision."

Kate smiled. "Wow! Thank you, Mrs. Bush!"

Laurie was recognized next. "Yes, this is a question for the first Mrs. Bush: How truly wonderful was Millie?"

"Now *that's* a question. Thank you, dear," said the elder Mrs. Bush. "Well, as all of you know, *Millie's Book* sold a tremendous number of copies. This was because she was a cute, pretty, and *very* obedient dog. And because a certain grandmother with pearls did the writing for her."

The press corps were besides themselves with the giggles, furiously writing down everything she said. I could just imagine Mr. Peabody's anger at that kind of condescending statement.

Barbara Bush continued. "As many of you may know, Bill Farish, the ambassador to England, gave us Millie. He was managing my Georgie's blind trust at the time and we went to visit him on his Kentucky horse farm. God, that place was fantastic. Makes this place look like Abu Ghraib. Anyway, not long afterward Georgie and I went quail-shooting at Farish's ten-thousand-acre ranch in Beeville, Texas—I know quail's big across the pond," she said with a nod to Stephen King. "Well, it was there that we decided to mate Millie with one of his prized spaniel—"

"ENOUGH!"

There was silence. Gambia Baraka, clad in a flowing dashiki and traditional *kanga* headscarf, had stood.

"On behalf of those without voices, I say ENOUGH!" Gambia's hands were dramatically raised and she looked skyward.

Candy turned to me. "Look for Tom Ridge to come bursting through the doors any second now."

Gambia lowered her arms, then fixed her gaze at not Barbara, but Laura Bush, and began a fiery soliloquy: "How can you, Mrs. Bush, a woman who professes to minister on behalf of the weakest among us, submit to the shackles—the shackles, I say, of this whitocracy? A slave-owning devil-ridden monetocratic coldheartocracy! Do you not hear the spirit calling you to break free, Laura Bush, break FREE, I say! Because like a caged bird no more, you cannot ignore the CHAINS holding you back, Laura Bush. It is TIME, Laura Bush." She had risen to a fever pitch. "And if I must slay you to free you, Laura Bush, then that I will do. Because, Laura Bush, IT IS TIME TO BE SET FREE!!!"

The doors did fly open and two ATF officers stormed in. And not too soon, since Gambia had blatantly threatened the First Lady. Mr. Zo was hiding behind Amy Tan.

But Laura Bush motioned for the officers to stand back. Instead the younger Mrs. Bush walked toward Gambia and grabbed both her hands.

"Gambia," she said with an almost glassy-eyed serenity, "that was absolutely beautiful. The passion you bring to your life's work inspires in all of us a journey of discovery that can only lead to a better place. We all thank you."

There was an extremely tense silence before tears began welling up in Gambia's eyes. She suddenly embraced Laura Bush.

"Oh, Mrs. Bush, I want so to reject the goodness of you," Gambia cried. "But the spirit won't allow me!"

"Just cry it out, Gambia, cry it out. I'm here for ya'," the First Lady said.

Barbara Bush, who throughout the tirade just stared at Gambia with a look of calmed bemusement, simply shook her iced tea glass. "If you're finished," she said to Gambia, "could you freshen me up? And don't forget the lemon." Before Gambia could react, a shout went up from David Gregory.

"Sacre bleu! C'est Barney!"

It was in fact Barney, who came trotting through the open doors.

"Well, look who's here," said Laura Bush, crouching over and clapping her hands for Barney to approach. The dog began crossing the room to meet her but when he was only halfway across, he stopped and stared—right at me.

"Here, Barney," said the First Lady, but Barney wasn't moving.

"Okay, people, hello-o? Who's he looking at?" asked Norah O'Donnell. Photographers were snapping away but Barney kept staring ahead, at me. What's more, he looked like he needed to say something, desperately.

I pushed between Terry Moran and Jonathan Alter—now wearing a neck brace—and impulsively went down on all fours and began crawling toward Barney. One of the armed guards began moving toward the dog from the opposite direction. And yet Barney didn't move at all. His eyes were still fixed on me. I accelerated my pace, as did the guard. It was a race to the dog.

Just as the guard began drawing his weapon, I pulled right up to Barney, my face against his. "What is it, Barney? What are you trying to tell me?" I said, not in cloying doggy-baby-talk, but like a prosecutor whose witness is finally ready to speak.

The laughter that rose from the press corps instantly shifted to gasps when the guard's weapon came up against my temple. I could hear Laura Bush rushing over to ease the standoff.

"Officer," she asked gently, "may I offer you something to read?" I ignored it all while I was face to face with Barney.

The President's Scottie looked me right in the eye, then gave out four barks. They were distinctive barks, the last one almost a whimper. Phonetically it would be written something like this: "Derrrr Thay Grrrib Curiooo." Of course, the "L" and "S" sounds are notoriously difficult for Scotties. With that in mind, I immediately reduced Barney's sounds to the closest English words and repeated them back to him.

"Daresay . . . glib . . . curio?" I asked. But by that time Gordon Johndroe had pushed the guard back and swooped up Barney in his arms.

I was left on all fours—and expecting another angry call on my cell from Eric within the next ten minutes. The only other thing I noticed was Laurie Dhue staring at me coldly—an expression I'd never before seen from her.

"I'll tell you one thing," said Barbara Bush. "Millie never would have created this kind of fracas. Now would someone please get me my iced tea?"

21

Vest in Show

There were three things that I had expected would happen immediately: Firstly Eric Sorenson called to confirm that, yes, I had committed strike two and I had one chance left before my press credentials were stripped. Secondly my East Room antic made the CNN and Fox News crawls and I became a pariah in the press corps. Even Candy started avoiding me.

So it came as a pleasant surprise that Thirdly—Laura Bush asking for my exile to Guantánamo Bay under the third Patriot Act— did not come to pass. She told the ATF agents that I was "simply enthusiastic, like a child with his very first book, alive with curiosity." She even sent me a copy of *The Brothers Karamazov* written for children.

The next day I paid a visit to Scott McClellan in his office, which lay tucked between the Briefing Room and the West Wing offices. I came to request a private sit-down interview with Barney.

After he finished laughing, I asked again. "You know, Scott, you may think I don't deserve a one-on-one with Barney after what happened yesterday. And I can understand that, I suppose. But it doesn't look very good when Fox News is the *only* network that ever gets access to the First Dog. There's an election coming up and it might behoove you to spread the wealth."

Even in my compromised state I could prick Scott on this point. "That's not fair!" he shot back.

"Or balanced, I know, but one has to ask why nobody other than Laurie Dhue gets access."

Scott averted his glance, then began shuffling papers on his desk. "Well, Mo, right now there are special restrictions on Barney."

"Restrictions?"

"That's right, so I'm afraid you can't see him." Scott still wouldn't look at me directly.

"Well, what kind of restrictions? Scott, this is my beat. I should know."

Scott finished messing with his papers, then looked me right in the eye. "Perhaps if you'd read Bob Novak's column this morning, Mo, you'd know that Barney has rickets."

"What?!" Rickets, a disease marked by the softening of the bones, was the result of malnutrition.

"I don't know anything else, so don't ask." Scott anxiously resumed his shuffling. He seemed nervous.

"Scott! You can't just drop something like that and expect me to not ask questions. Dammit, what's going on? Barney looked perfectly fine yesterday."

"Apparently someone leaked it," he said. "All I know is that it's true."

I hadn't read Novak's column that day. "Gee, I can't imagine who leaked it."

"Neither can I," said Scott, almost defiantly. "Now if you please." He picked up his stack and moved toward a thin closet just by the office door. I couldn't let him leave just yet so I stepped between him and the closet.

Scott lowered his chin. "Now, Mo, you don't want to make me late." He shot a glance toward the doorway. Gephardt the Albino was standing right there, looming, arms crossed and menacing. I instinctively moved away, barely able to suppress a shudder.

Scott opened up the closet door and reached for his jacket. Inside, hanging next to the jacket, was a blue satin vest.

"That's the famous press secretary's vest, isn't it?" I asked. The legendary vest had been passed from secretary to secretary. Supposedly there was a note placed in the inside pocket and passed down. The contents of that note were unknown to anyone else.

Gephardt the Albino shot me an arctic-cold stare.

Scott shut the closet door and put on his jacket. "Your mother must have had a tough time keeping your hand out of the cookie jar," he said without affection. "Sorry this meeting had to end so abruptly."

Once again I left with more questions than answers. Whether or not Barney actually had rickets, this felt eerily like an attempt to push him out of the public's view altogether. It was something that Mr. Peabody had suggested might happen.

22

Dick Morris's Feet

Any good reporter has more than one source for a big story. And this was turning out to be the biggest story I'd ever hoped to cover.

I'd chosen to believe the core of what Helen and Mr. Peabody had told me. Pets and Presidents, I was willing to accept, were tied to each other by virtue of an ancient pact originating with Cincinnatus and his horse Sadie. To this day the President received advice from his pet.

But the inner circle surrounding the President jealously guarded their influence with the Commander-in-Chief. Over time the pet had become marginalized and the clueless press had long ceased to offer protection. Now if the pet tried to fulfill its true responsibilities it faced grave danger. In Barney's case, the rickets leak might very well be more than rumor. I needed to ratchet up my investigation.

My first instinct was to track down Bob Novak. But he was tied down all day at the Fox-sponsored second annual *Culture War Games*. The event was, I had to admit, great television. Where else could you see Pat Robertson in a tank top? I had to tune in for at least a few minutes.

Team Traditionalist once again boasted an impressive roster. Conservative Congresswoman Marilyn Musgrave and Bob Jones III were unbeatable at the three-legged race. And the *Washington Times*'s Tony Blankley ran the tires like nobody's business.

Team Secularist was more of a hodgepodge—liberal thinkers, sitcom actors, convicted rappers, and child molesters all lumped together by Fox News. Team captain Eric Alterman, from *The Nation* magazine, objected to the composition of his team. But Team Traditionalist captain Bill O'Reilly was having none of it, "If you're not a traditionalist, you're a secularist, Alterman," he bellowed, jabbing his finger with Robert Conrad–like fury into Alterman's chest. "So stop your whining."

Team Secularist actually put up a decent fight. Naomi Wolf and Ludacris won the wheelbarrow race but then Dr. Laura Schlessinger tied it up with a lightning-fast performance on the monkey bars, after which Dr. James Dobson dumped a bucket of ice-cold Gatorade on her head in celebration.

Time was wasting, though. I turned off the TV and got back to work.

I needed to seek out someone who might have the goods on a former presidential pet and a very mysterious incident.

Buddy, Bill Clinton's four-year old chocolate Lab, was killed in January of 2002, less than a year after moving to Chappaqua. All that was known was that a seventeen-year-old girl, driving on a busy Route 117, struck Buddy, who'd reportedly been chasing after a van that had just left the Clintons' property.

The Internet had become rife with conspiracy theories about the death. Some speculated that Mrs. Clinton's former press secretary Maggie Williams had poisoned the dog with chocolate, then placed his body in the road to make it look like an accident. (Indeed traces of chocolate were found in both Buddy's *and* Vince Foster's bodies.) Maggie Williams, according to these sources, was also responsible for the death of Kurt Cobain. She apparently spent most of her time outside of the office.

What happened, I wondered, to Buddy and to his predecessor Socks the cat, whose exile from the West Wing was equally suspicious? I wasn't interested in hysterical speculation. For sober perspective I sought out former Clinton advisor Dick Morris.

I had only met Dick once before, at New York's Peninsula Hotel spa. I had been given a gift certificate for a deep-tissue massage. Dick was at the Peninsula for his weekly pedicure. He'd just successfully undergone "toe cleavage" surgery.

"They just shortened a couple of toes and lopped off a bunion," he had explained. "Jimmy Choo is coming out with a men's line and damn if I'm not going to squeeze into them," he had said.

It was early March 2001 so the Bush administration was less than two months old and people were still talking about the alleged trashing of the West Wing by outgoing Clinton staffers.

Dick had claimed to have the inside scoop: "You do realize what really happened, don't you? Bill Clinton invited some Arkansas state troopers over for his bon voyage. Naturally they brought along a busload of strippers. Things got out of control and everyone, including the President, started pouring Bartles & Jaymes wine coolers on the computer keyboards. Anyone can tell you that that destroys even the finest electronics."

"I'm not sure I believe that the President would do that," I had said.

"Don't kid yourself, I worked for Bill Clinton in the White House. I know how vindictive the man can be and I know his dietary habits. Who else do you think it was who smeared Big Mac special sauce all over the bust of Lincoln in the Oval Office? As I told Bill O'Reilly, the defacement of that image is an impeachable offense."

"But Clinton was already impeached. How do you know any of this anyway? You broke with the Clintons long ago."

"Just trust me. Hey, careful with the padding," he had snipped at the pedicurist. "There's fresh collagen in there."

This time around I caught up with Dick at the swanky Ilo Day Spa on Wisconsin Avenue in Georgetown. Ilo had been frequented by many high-profile Washingtonians, Monica Lewinsky and Tipper Gore, to name just a couple.

I found Dick getting a mud bath, his face covered by a towel. I sank into the next tub of mud before I called out to him.

"Well, if it isn't Mo Rocca. I read about your escapade in the East Room. You must have your tail between your legs," he snickered. "What are you doing here?" Every time I saw Dick I couldn't help but think of what a great Mordred he'd make in a revival of *Camelot*. But I needed to stay focused.

"I'm here to detoxify," I lied. "And I thought I might catch up with you."

"Well, you've come to the right place. The peat-moss volcanic ash blend can't be beat. And the sloughing you'll get! Before I started coming here, I had skin rougher than Noriega's."

"Interesting. So, Dick, I've been thinking. It's coming up on three years since Clinton's Lab Buddy died. It seemed innocent enough. Do you think there was any bigger story behind it?"

"Chico," Dick called over to his young Mexican attendant. *"Mas, por favor."* The attendant poured a couple of fresh buckets of mud on Dick as he began holding forth. "Let's be very clear about this. Nothing with the Clintons is as simple as it seems. There's always a bigger story.

"Remember that *Governor* Clinton's dog Zeke was similarly killed in 1990 in Little Rock," he continued. "Mysteriously run over *after* Clinton had been successfully reelected."

"You're suggesting that the Clintons didn't need Zeke anymore?"

"I don't suggest. I merely state facts. Chico, *agua,*" he directed the serving boy. He turned back to me. "Remember also that Buddy the Lab was acquired in December 1997, shortly before the Lewinsky scandal surfaced. The dog was certain to make Clinton more popular."

"You mean Clinton knew that he'd be in legal hot water soon and wanted the dog as a diversion for the public?"

"*Gracias,*" Dick said to the boy. He took a swig of water before Chico placed two fresh cucumber slices on Dick's eyes. "A diversion? Like the bombing of a Sudanese aspirin factory? I would *never* accuse the Clintons of something like that." He laughed.

"Very interesting," I said. "And what about Socks?"

Dick flinched. Although I couldn't see his eyes, I could tell he was bothered by the question. "What do you mean, 'what about Socks'?"

"Well, Socks the cat was suspiciously exiled from the White House and placed under the supervision of Betty Currie and away from the press not long after Buddy's grand entrance. Whose decision was that?"

Clinton's cat Socks complaining to presidential secretary Betty Currie about changes in the White House, post-'94 midterms.

"I don't know," he said abruptly. "The two pets probably didn't get along. So it was probably Buddy's 'decision,' as you say." Dick laughed nervously.

Something wasn't sitting right. "No," I said, "something tells me that Buddy's the patsy here. Something or someone else forced Socks to relinquish power."

Dick was squirming in his mud. "Chico, bring me my bath sheet!" Dick stood up as Chico wiped him off. I looked away as quickly as possible. "I'm afraid the heat is getting to you, Mo." Dick wrapped himself in Egyptian cotton, balanced himself on Chico, then ever so carefully stepped into his cashmere bunny slippers, grabbed his man-bag, and turned to me. "You know, when I hear wackos like you, I lose all faith in the system."

23

When Good Presidential Pets Go Bad

"I hope I didn't compromise you in any way, Helen, but I needed to investigate on my own," I said. Helen, Mr. Peabody, and I were all sitting in Helen's lair. Today was Helen's molting day so she needed to take it easy.

"I believe I told you to be discreet," sniffed Mr. Peabody, who was brushing out Helen's old feathers and collecting them in a pile on the floor. "It is extremely important that you give no one the sense that you may be privy to this kind of information." Mr. Peabody was unusually agitated on this point.

"Now, now, Mr. Peabody," said Helen, "I would never want Mo to accept the first answer he's given. That would be shoddy reporting."

"As you like it, Madame," said Mr. Peabody.

"Thanks for understanding," I said. "I guess I just needed to see how different theories stack up."

"Or you could just look at primary source material on the Clinton presidency," said Helen. "Remember, all you have to do is ask. Mr. Peabody?"

Mr. Peabody handed me a copy of *All Too Feline,* an unpublished tell-all memoir by Socks the cat. The introduction was all I needed to read:

> I was such an idealist when I first came to the White House. The Clintons were my kind of people, passionate about ideas and reform. We were going to change the world.
>
> When I told the President to back the Oslo peace process with its prudent exclusion of any decision on the status of Jerusalem, he went ahead and invited Arafat and Rabin to the Rose Garden. When I told Mrs. Clinton about my urinary tract infection, she launched an unsuccessful but well-intentioned initiative for universal health care. All in all our first year in office was mixed, but we were optimistic.
>
> I could overlook some of the President's foibles, like his Hollywood friends who were overrunning the place. Did Markie Post really deserve a private briefing on Haiti? What did Ted Danson really know about Somalia? It seemed at times that Linda Bloodworth-Thomason was the chief of staff. Please. *Designing Women* might have been a hit, but *Evening Shade*? Total crap. I can't believe that Charles Durning and Marilu Henner embarrassed themselves by appearing on that dud. You knew they'd really jumped the shark when Kenny Rogers made a cameo.
>
> But then something happened that marked a darker shift. After the '94 midterm elections, a new kind of presidential advisor entered the scene. A practitioner of political black arts, a Svengali, also known as the Political Consultant. His name was Dick Morris and his first order of business was to exile me to the East Wing. Soon my role as First Pet wasn't worth a bowl of warm drool. Then one morning, after one of his mysterious overnight polls, he advised the President to co-opt the "Millie vote" by getting a dog—this he called triangulation. (Overnight polls? Who the hell answers the phone at 4 A.M. to answer Dick Morris's questions?)
>
> In the end nothing was sacred, except of course that tartan dog bowl that I'd occasionally find press secretary Mike McCurry caressing.

"The manuscript caused quite some consternation in the Clinton camp," said Mr. Peabody. "Mrs. Clinton never forgave him. But Socks felt he needed to write about some of the problems he saw in the White House."

"It serves as a cautionary tale for White House pets who may enter office with high expectations," said Helen. "They're entering in an increasingly precarious time."

"Socks didn't allow himself to get used," I said. "But are there good presidential pets who have gone bad?"

"Of course," said Helen. "None of the American presidential pets have gone so far as, say, Hitler's sheepdog Blondie. That said, all too often a counselor to a president—someone who should give candid advice—has become a willing prop or shill for the administration."

"That was Buddy's role, I'm afraid," said Mr. Peabody. "To be a distraction in a swirl of scandal. He was not, by the way, murdered. So Mr. Scaife, if you're reading this, you can recall your private investigators from the Chappaqua Pet Morgue. Buddy's death was an accident."

"The death of Warren Harding's Airedale Laddie Boy wasn't so accidental," Helen said. "He too had cheapened his office by doing exactly what the administration wanted—playing it cute for the press, sitting in a specially built chair in the Cabinet room for mock interviews with the *Washington Star*. It was adorable, all right, and it helped steal focus from the Teapot Dome scandal. After Harding died in 1923, Laddie Boy felt so guilty for shirking his responsibility that he killed himself."

Mr. Peabody picked up here. "Then there are the pets who have enabled presidential inaction or delinquency, like James Buchanan's Newfie Lara. President Buchanan spent most of his ill-fated term in a state of emotional crisis over his breakup with former vice president William Rufus King. Lara simply—"

"Wait a minute, Mr. Peabody!" I said. "You're not implying that

Warren Harding's self-loathing airedale, Laddie Boy, shortly before his sad end.

President Buchanan was gay. I've been to his estate Wheatland. I've heard all about the death of his first love, Ann Coleman. He was so heartbroken he was never able to love again." The docent had nearly brought my mother and me to tears telling us that story.

"James Buchanan was about as straight as Dudley Do-Right," said Mr. Peabody dismissively. "He lived with Mr. King when the two were senators. When King, then V.P. under Pierce, died after sailing to Cuba for vacation in 1853, Buchanan lost his marbles."

"Sailing to Cuba? I didn't know they had gay cruises back then," I chuckled.

Mr. Peabody gave me a withering stare. "I'm sorry, but open-mike night was last night."

Laddie Boy's last note.

"Bitch," I muttered under my breath.

"Buchanan went into a years-long tailspin," continued Mr. Peabody. "Before seven southern states seceded in the last months of his term, Buchanan should have been making some hard decisions. That's what the Chief Executive is supposed to do. Instead he was going out till all hours on Dupont Circle, doing God knows what at clubs like Man-T-Bellums, hoping problems would solve themselves. It didn't help that he was high as a kite on wormwood poppers."

"Major antebellum party drug," explained Helen ruefully. "Lara helped him procure it."

I glanced over at the infamous photograph of Jimmy Carter in a rowboat in a Plains lake, wielding his oar toward what he claimed was a rabbit menacingly swimming at him. The whole incident contributed to Carter's image as ineffectual in the face of any threat.

"You're interested in the 'Killer Bunny' story," surmised Helen. "Jody Powell really saved him on that one."

"Saved him?!" I said. Powell, Carter's press secretary, had casually mentioned the April 1979 incident to AP reporter Brooks Jackson the following August, then lived to regret it when the

President Carter ready to defend himself against a suicide (or homicide) nutria.

whole press picked up on it. This was hardly a favor. "Powell ended up giving the press and the Republicans a perfect way to make Carter look foolish."

"You do learn slowly," sighed Mr. Peabody. "Powell averted a major crisis. First of all the animal was in fact a nutria."

"A nutria?" I asked. "You mean the reddish brown semiaquatic fourteen-inch-long rodent with webbed hind feet and razor-sharp teeth for cutting through plants?"

"Yes, the one with the cylindrical, sparsely haired tail and soft gray under-fur that in fact can grow to a length of three feet." Mr. Peabody always needed to top me. "Kenny had been a presidential pet, living at the family's compound in Plains, Georgia, before falling under the spell of the Ayatollah Khomeini and becoming a radical Islamist. Out of safety concerns the Carter family expelled the nutria, renamed Khalid, which unfortunately remained in the area. Classified intelligence suggested that if given the chance, the nutria would do everything in its power to harm Carter. Diplomacy would not likely work."

"So Carter had to use the oar," I said. "But why would the administration intentionally leak this story?"

"To preempt a more damaging version of the story if it leaked through another source. Jody Powell knew the whole incident had the potential of revealing the power of pets. He rightly decided that marginalizing the animal with the mock sobriquet 'killer bunny' would cast the whole story in a 'kooky animal tale' light that the administration could live with," said Mr. Peabody.

"Those press secretaries are crafty," said Helen. "They share their secrets only with each other."

"That's right," I said. "Speaking of which, do either of you know what's written in the note passed on through the traditional press secretary vest?"

"Oh, that is something that even I'm not privy to," said Helen.

Mr. Peabody remained silent on this count, then suddenly spoke up. "I really must continue cataloging," he said. "Madame, if I may."

"That's fine, Tad." (Tad apparently was Mr. Peabody's first name.) "Mo can stay with me while I finish molting."

Mr. Peabody receded into the darkness. It was the first time I'd had alone with Helen in a few days.

"I'm sorry Mr. Peabody was a little sharp with you. Sometimes he gets very tense, I don't know why." Helen walked over to her refrigerator. "Can I offer you something to eat?" Helen asked, pulling out a Tupperware container of beaver carrion.

"I've already eaten, thank you. Helen, I have to tell you again how grateful I am for all you've divulged to me. But again, I have to ask why. Why me?"

"Mo, let's be realistic. I'm over two hundred years old. I'll be lucky if I live another forty. Someone outside the White House—someone other than I—needs to know about the Presidential Pet line. It's the surest way to guarantee its survival. And that's immensely important—because without its survival, we lose an invaluable ingredient of good governance. Presidents need counsel—smart, honest, commonsense counsel. Without this 'sacred animal' ingredient, leadership is in a terrible state of imbalance. The executive becomes arrogant, drunk with its own sense of invulnerability. President Eisenhower came to understand this at the end of his presidency when he warned us about the 'potential for the disastrous rise of *misplaced power.*' "

"I thought he was talking about the military-industrial complex," I said.

" 'Military-industrial complex'? Never heard of it, but I'm sure it's an anagram for something pet-related," Helen said with a shrug.

"So what do you want me to do with all this?" I asked. "Just carry this with me?"

"I want you to write it down, in a history that once and for all can be read by everyone."

"You mean no one else has tried?"

"Others have tried," Helen conceded. "Henry Adams gave it a shot. It was too literary. I considered Edmund Morris but he just kept procrastinating. I thought of Gore Vidal but he's a historical *fiction* writer. You really can't believe anything he writes. So the task now falls to you."

She continued. "One day they may find these archives and destroy them. Then all evidence of the 'sacred animal' will be destroyed and we'll be all the poorer."

"Helen, this is a challenge I didn't expect. For me to commit my name to this. Why wouldn't you just—"

"*Please* don't ask why I don't write it. Just trust me that much depends on you rising to this. And if you ever doubt the importance of presidential pets," she said, "consider the story of FDR's Fala and Churchill's Rufus."

What she handed me then was not the transcript of a Fala fireside chat (that would have been way too obvious), but a speech by Winston Churchill's chocolate poodle Rufus. It was his eulogy to Fala:

> In remembering Fala, one thinks of Marvell's line on the untimely end of Charles I: "He nothing common did or mean/Upon that memorable scene . . ." The scene of our meeting was the deck of the USS *Augusta* in the second year of war.
>
> Spirited from lapping up the runoff of Pol Roger streaming out of the President and Prime Minister's dining cabin, our bond took on a heady exuberance. Heady, until I slipped and plopped right into the cold northern waters.
>
> Not a human could hear my cries, and the fish were of little use. Now, it seemed, had come my darkest hour. It was in that bleakest of moments that Fala risked all, diving in and delivering me to safety by the scruff of my neck.
>
> From that day forth he committed himself to the welfare of me and my people—and I to him and his people. A common interest and common destiny.
>
> Though the story became one of humans conquering evil, it began with a sniff. I knew from the very first whiff of that great Scottie's behind that he was far from common. And so I say . . .
>
> In War: Resolution
>
> In Defeat: Defiance
>
> In Victory: Magnanimity
>
> In Peace: Goodwill
>
> In Friendship: Fala

It was a beautiful passage. Helen took my hand in her claw.

"I want you to have something. No one—not even Mr. Peabody—knows I possess it. There is something known as the Fala Grail. There are three parts. The first is Fala's dog bowl."

"Is that what Socks was referring to in his book?"

"That's right. The second is Fala's dog collar. We don't know where that is." Then she moved over to the Houdon bust of herself. "The third is his favorite chew toy."

Helen carefully lifted the bust and pulled out a chewed-up plastic Pinocchio toy. She placed it in my hand. "I want you to have it. It is extremely valuable."

It was so small and yet it felt magical in my palm. A tiny chewed-up plastic relic.

FDR's Scottie Fala and his Pinocchio chew toy, the final piece of the coveted Fala Grail.

"Why is it so important?" I asked.

"Those radicals around the president—those who oppose the humane counsel of the 'sacred animal'—believe that if they can obtain all three parts, they can once and for all assume the power and influence that Fala had." She became grim here. "And then the real presidential pet will finally be rendered obsolete, stripped of its nation-saving power . . . dispensable."

"Oh, Helen, I'm overwhelmed. But I just don't know if I can write this—"

"Please," she said. "As you think about what I'm asking, think about Fala. And think about Barney."

I had one last question. "Helen, Barney doesn't really have rickets, does he? I'm guessing it's just a rumor spread to undermine him, just like when Truman's Irish setter Mike was supposedly sent away for the same reason?"

"You're right about Barney, wrong about Mike. He really did have rickets. The Dixiecrats force-fed him candy as punishment after he convinced Truman to integrate the armed forces."

My brain hurting from yet another factoid, I set out.

24

Eyes Wide Open

I needed some time alone to sort things out.

I climbed up from Helen's lair and out from under her desk. Even though it was late at night, I chose to exit through Helen's desk downstairs in the pressroom. I just couldn't deal with the gutter right now. Besides, reporters often stayed late into the night, so the security guard would think nothing of it if I left through the gate.

I nearly tripped over Helen's Easy Spirits, then climbed the steps into the Briefing Room area. I was about to walk straight out onto the North Lawn when I heard what sounded like a soft wail. It was coming from the direction of Scott's office, behind the Briefing Room.

As I tiptoed closer the wailing got louder. Scott certainly wouldn't be working this late. Maybe an animal had made its way in and was trapped. As I neared his office, I could see that his door was only open a crack and a soft light flickered from inside. The noise from the office was much fuller now. The wailing I could hear was a woman's voice, not an animal's, and it was joined by the lower-registered moans of men—a few of them.

The collective sound was both vaguely religious, almost chant-like, and unmistakably sexual.

Ever so carefully I pressed my chest against the wall, just beside the door's crack, then crept as slowly as possible, leading with my head, toward the opening. I stopped once I had a clear view. I felt sufficiently cloaked in darkness to stay for a good long look.

What I saw shocked me.

Inside, illuminated by a single candle on Scott's desk, stood a circle of nine individuals. They were clad in white robes, monk-like cowls, with hoods concealing their heads. What appeared to be six full-grown men swayed and moaned, their palms facing up. One woman sang out. There was also one midget of inde-terminate gender and one Sasquatch-size individual, presumably another man.

As they grew more excited, their bodies undulating, their heads nodding, the hoods began inching back from their faces. I could see now that the ritual participants included Scott McClellan, White House advisor Karl Rove, Fox News chief Roger Ailes, former press secretary Ari Fleischer, Senator Zell Miller, and Gephardt the Albino. When the hood dropped back from the head of the giant, I was shocked to see White House counselor Karen Hughes.

The midget's identity was still hidden by his or her hood.

The lone average-size woman began rocking back and forth so passionately that the hood flew back completely from her face. It was Laurie Dhue, her lips glistening more than ever, her eyes widening. She was panting heavily by now, between high-pitched wails.

Then something strange happened. Scott slowly entered the circle, drawn there it seemed by his co-ritualists' calls. As the oth-ers began growing louder and closing in on him, Scott began removing his robe. He pulled it over his head. Laurie was screaming like a banshee now as Scott threw the robe aside. It was almost as if Laurie was an audience member at some satanic Chippendales show.

I had barely a second to imagine another facile pop-culture comparison, though, when I noticed what Scott had revealed.

A pantless Scott McClellan was wearing only the ceremonial Press Secretary's vest. He began dancing, a man apparently possessed, as Laurie's shrieks grew wilder. It was a strange agitated dance, as if he were checking himself for fleas. He scratched himself with his hands and his feet, then shook his butt in the direction of each of the others. It was really more of a wagging motion. (Scott's right ass cheek, by the way, was tattooed with the letters "P.S." My assumption was that the letters stood not for "Priore de Sion" but for "press secretary.") Each of the others exaggeratedly sniffed in the direction of Scott's butt.

Finally Scott lifted a drinking cup. It looked like a very wide-rimmed chalice, but one without a stem—really almost a bowl, a tartan bowl. It was Fala's bowl! He grandly drank from it. When he was done he took a deep breath and howled.

Then Gephardt the Albino reached with his left arm underneath his right sleeve and from the upper arm removed a dog collar. It was Fala's dog collar! He carefully attached it to Scott's neck. Scott howled again, this time even more loudly.

At this point Laurie, worked up into her own ecstatic frenzy, let out a climactic yowl and collapsed onto the floor. The others began dancing around her.

I was terrified and yet I couldn't contain myself. "The Grail!" I said, just loudly enough that the still-concealed midget looked up at me, then down at my hand—at the Pinocchio chew toy!

There was no time to think. Only time to run.

25

The Great Hallucinator?

I burst through the doors, never once looking back, and ran straight for the security gate. I must have looked dazed because the guard asked if everything was okay as I stumbled onto Pennsylvania Avenue. I couldn't answer, I was in such a state of shock.

It was three-thirty in the morning and I'd just witnessed a terrifying scene. Worse yet, I'd been seen with the Fala chew toy. I needed to talk to somebody, anybody.

I ran down Pennsylvania Avenue, not knowing where I might end up. It was freezing cold and the street was empty, except of course for Condoleezza Rice, who was doing her midmorning sprints. She was so "in the zone," she didn't notice me.

I ended up at Candy's apartment building in the Adams Morgan neighborhood and pressed down on the buzzer. There was no response.

"Candy, where are you?"

I kept pressing until she finally buzzed me into the lobby. I ran up six flights, pushing past a meth dealer and two prostitutes, until I came to her apartment. I rapped loudly on the door. Barely awake, she opened it a crack, only as far as the chain would let it. She was dressed in a purple robe, her hair piled messily on top (a look Candy herself called "sex hair"). Even at this hour she stood in her trademark three-quarter-turned position.

"Candy, something terrible is happening." I was breathless. "I've got to talk to you."

Candy looked skeptical. "It's not a good time, kiddo."

"Look, Candy," I said. "I know that Pasquale is in there with you, but *I* need you right now."

"Pasquale? I think you mean Alonzo."

"Whatever, Candy. I'm in crisis. *Please.*"

Candy wouldn't look me in the eye. "Listen, Mo, things have been getting a little too weird with you. First the pussy talk with President Fox. Then the all-fours routine with the First Lady."

"Caaaan-dy," beckoned a Latin voice from inside.

"Bring it down a notch, hot stuff," shouted back Candy. Then she looked at me again. "Sorry, Mo. I just can't do this anymore."

It hurt her to do it but she closed the door on me. The last thing I heard was Candy yelling back to Alonzo: "Looks like Carnivale's getting started early this year!"

There wasn't time to mourn the loss of my friendship with Candy. I tore down the steps, nearly trampling an old Guatemalan woman selling carnations, and started running as fast as I could along the Potomac River toward the Maryland suburbs. It was 4 A.M. now. The only sound I could hear was Condoleezza Rice swimming laps across the Potomac.

I wasn't in great shape so I didn't make it to Wolf's house in Bethesda until daybreak at 6 A.M. I kicked off my shoes and started clanging his chimes frantically.

Mihoko the ancient serving girl opened the door. I pushed past her and ran out back.

I stopped dead in my tracks. "Oh my God, Wolf!" I felt like I'd been cheated on. There in his backyard Wolf was teaching kendo, the art of Japanese fencing, to Anderson Cooper.

Wolf turned to me. He wasn't smiling.

"Wolf, I need to talk to you," I said.

Wolf put down his wooden sword, or *bokken,* then turned to Anderson to ask for a moment. *"Chotto Matte Kudasai."*

"Hai," Anderson assented with a quick bow.

Wolf walked over to me, looking grim. "What's up, Mo-san?" he asked curtly.

"Wolf, I'm in trouble. Big trouble. There's a group of people at the White House. They might try to hurt Barney. And now they might try to hurt me. I need you now more than ever."

"I'm sorry, Mo-san, but you are not welcome here."

"Why?"

"Your recent behavior has dishonored both yourself and your sensei. Our very own CNN poll shows that 91 percent of the American people believe you are a danger to Barney. The margin of error is only 3 percent."

"I'm a danger?! Oh, Wolf, what happened to us?" I looked over at Anderson, who was studiously practicing his lunges. "He's even wearing my *dogi,"* I added wistfully, using the Japanese word for "uniform."

"Mihoko will see you out," Wolf said stonily.

I started to walk out when Wolf's Akita puppy gamboled out from the house.

"Ki O Tsukete, Aaron!" ("Be careful, Aaron!"), yelled Wolf, scared that I might harm the little dog. Wolf scooped the puppy up in his arms as Anderson leaped between us, twirling his sword in my face.

"It's *not* a baton," I hissed before turning and marching out.

As I walked out through the front door, Mihoko let go one parting shot—"Don't let door hit in ass on way out!"—before slamming it shut.

Rejected by two of the people I thought I could rely on, I had one last place to go. I ran back downtown to visit with the man I looked up to more than any other.

Abraham Lincoln. Daniel Chester French gave me an icon to

which I could pray without any compunction. No one could ever call him a false idol.

I got there at 7 A.M. Condi had just finished rappelling off the Washington Monument and was doing her cool-down javelin throws. She jogged off, probably to begin her rounds on the Sunday news shows.

A couple hundred yards away late-night straggler Ann Coulter was hiking across the lawn barefoot in a skimpy black cocktail dress talking with Hannity. Colmes trailed behind, holding her high heels.

"Oh, please!" she scowled. "Lincoln was about as Republican as Bill Weld."

Once they'd passed I was alone, the Mall desolate. I walked to the top of the memorial's steps and looked up at Lincoln. It was just the two of us, and I instantly felt calmed. I held in my hand the Fala chew toy, perhaps the only thing standing between the safety of the presidential pet and a complete takeover by the President's inner circle of radical Barney opponents. So much was at stake and while I was no believer in voices from the dead, I held out hope that maybe some answers would come to me if I meditated long enough.

I got down on my knees and bowed my head. "Oh, Mr. President," I whispered, "what has happened to the White House? You were just a simple rail-splitter from Hardin County, Kentucky, born in 1809 to undistinguished parentage. But you were an honest and wise leader with a diverse Cabinet that you listened to. It was a glorious intellectual ferment, a constant exchange of ideas. You actually engaged the press in a rich dialogue. Your correspondence with Horace Greeley about the Union and slavery—"

I would have continued but when I looked up, something miraculous had happened. Lincoln's right thumb and forefinger were reconfigured in an "L" shape on his forehead.

"Mr. President!"

Then something even more magical happened. Lincoln spoke. "Sorry, guy," he said, "but someone needs a reality check." He had a high, thin voice. "I appointed a diverse Cabinet because I'd made campaign promises. And as for the press, I was a master manipulator. I offered one Democratic editor the post of minister to France just to get him off my back. And don't get me started on Greeley. I had to humor him since the guy was ripping me a new one every chance he got. He even called for my resignation at one point." Lincoln threw up his hands. "Give me a break!"

That Lincoln sounded like ABC's John Stossel was something of a letdown, but I was riveted by his words.

"Here's the thing: editorial writers know zip about running the country," Lincoln continued. "Don't get me wrong, I like that Tom Friedman fellow, even if the whole 'Arab street' line is a little played out," he added tartly.

"Well, no one created metaphors like you," I gushed. "By the way, can I tell you what a huge fan I am of your House Divided speech?"

"Thanks. I lost my Senate race after that so I've always been a little insecure about it."

"Anyway," I said, "I guess I am a little naive. You were a politician after all. You had to do some pretty unsavory things to get your way."

"No kidding. I suspended the right of habeas corpus, I imprisoned southern sympathizers without trial. This is true. But give me a break!" Once again I cringed. "I was trying to save the Union, folks! To give hope to the world for all future time, people. These were big-ticket items—not midnight basketball penny-ante b.s."

I hadn't planned on talking with Lincoln this night so I wasn't really prepared with questions. "I hope this isn't too personal, Mr. President, but I've read that you could sometimes get a little, well, gloomy. How did you get through it all?"

"Gloomy? Try bipolar," he said. "Of course it didn't help much that I married a lunatic. To stay focused and keep my spirits up I relied on my better angels," he said, referring to his first inaugural address. "And if you don't know who they are by now, you're more clueless than General McClellan. Better Angels, come on out."

Two goats galloped out from behind the statue.

"It's Nanny and Nanko!" I said. Nanny and Nanko were the rambunctious goats who belonged to Lincoln's youngest son. He used to attach kitchen chairs to the goats and ride them around the house.

"Those animals were smart. They knew that the best thing they could do was keep me entertained," said Lincoln as the goats took center stage and began doing a jig. Lincoln was in heaven.

"Mr. President," I said, "it's clear to me that every presidential pet has had a different way of serving its administration. I don't know much about Barney's strengths and weaknesses. But I fear for our country if he's not able to speak his mind to the current President. He may be our last best hope."

"Hey, good line. I share that opinion. But who am I? The world will little note nor long remember what I say here, but—"

"No, it won't!" echoed a deep and menacing voice.

Suddenly Lincoln's face clouded over!

"What's happening?" I yelled. A beautiful scene had just turned dangerous. I looked at Nanny and Nanko, who started bleating in terror. I turned back to Lincoln's statue. But as the cloud cleared, Lincoln was no more. The head on the statue was Richard Nixon's!

"Richard Nixon! What have you done with Lincoln?"

"Sorry, kid, but now he belongs to the ages—and he ain't coming back."

"What is it that you want?"

"You're a little too curious about presidential pets and I think you need to back off—or you'll get your skinny little tit caught in a wringer!"

"You stole that line from John Mitchell. Well guess what? I'm not scared of you. You always hated the press. And you did bad things. Okay, you also did some good things, like opening relations with China and starting the EPA. I believe the National Endowment of the Arts began under your watch as well." I wanted to be fair. "But you tried to make yourself unaccountable. Well, President Nixon, I'm no lapdog!"

"Now, now, let's relax." He leaned toward me. "There's no reason we can't be friends. Bebe! Get our friend a drink."

Suddenly Nixon's best friend, the Cuban American banker Bebe Rebozo, walked in. He was immaculately dressed in white trousers, Gucci loafers, and a guayabera linen shirt.

Bebe approached me with a mojito in hand. I couldn't see behind his sunglasses—the kind I'd always associated with Meyer Lansky—but I felt threatened, even if I was momentarily taken with his vintage Seiko.

"Please, have a mojito," he beckoned as he moved closer. Just then Checkers, Nixon's vice presidential dog, bounded out from behind the statue and began pulling on Bebe's pant leg with his teeth.

"Checkers," scowled Nixon, "get back from there!"

But Checkers wasn't obeying.

"Please, have the mojito," persisted Bebe as he moved still nearer, the dog futilely trying to hold him back. That's when I noticed Bebe slip a white powder into the drink and stir.

"No, thank you, Señor Rebozo. I'm fine."

Bebe was becoming more aggressive. "You like the mojito," he said hypnotically. I started backing up down the steps, determined not to be poisoned by Bebe Rebozo on the steps of this temple.

"No, really. Thank you, Bebe, but I'll pass."

"Mo-ji-to," he chanted.

I was walking backward down the steps more quickly and nearly tripped a couple of times. Bebe wasn't slowing down, though. At closer range I could see that behind his sunglasses he was eyeing my Fala chew toy. I clutched it even tighter.

I'd come to the bottom of the steps and continued walking backward, the pace still quickening. Bebe wasn't letting up.

"Checkers, get back here!" barked Nixon from his chair.

It was then that I decided to make a run for it. But as I turned around, I ran right into the edge of the Reflecting Pool. I teetered for a moment before regaining my balance, when a blinding whiteness came rushing in from my left. It came so quickly, I didn't have a chance to turn and see what it was barreling toward me. Suddenly a large cold hand gripped my neck from behind and plunged my face into the pool.

I'm not sure how long I was under because everything went black. I only heard voices—a stream of voices from the present and the past:

"You have dishonored yourself and your sensei," said Wolf.

"I'm sorry, Mo. I just can't do this anymore," said Candy.

" 'Swing low, sweet chariot,' " sang Marian Anderson.

"What's next, a memorial for Jim Jeffords?!" said Ann Coulter.

"Give me a break!" said Lincoln.

I assumed I'd passed on. It hadn't been such a bad life, I thought. A little on the short side, yes, but not if I'd been born in Bangladesh, where the life expectancy for men is forty-eight years. And let's face it, I never once had to deal with monsoon season.

Just as I was making peace with the humiliation of drowning in the two-foot-deep Reflecting Pool, someone grabbed the neck of my shirt and fished me out. It was Laurie Dhue.

"Oh, wow, Laurie!" I said, my vision blurred since my glasses had dropped to the bottom of the pool. "I think you saved me. Bebe Rebozo was going to poison me."

"Are we rolling?" said Laurie.

Before I could ask what she meant, the scene came into more of a focus. Laurie was filming me, and we were live.

"Yes, Shep, I'm live at the Mall and while I haven't got anything to report on Barney and his rickets, I am witnessing a tremendous moment of a different kind. Mo Rocca, an MSNBC reporter, known to the hundreds of people nationwide who sometimes watch that network, has gone over the brink. We're looking at the self-destruction of someone who one day might very well have found a job at CNNfn."

I was still disoriented. "Laurie, what's going on? Why are you doing this? The real story is Nixon. He's back. Just look up there."

I looked up the steps, squinting hard enough to see that it was Lincoln, not Nixon, in the Lincoln Memorial.

"It's sad, Shep, to see a comrade fallen in arms," said Laurie in her full-out "sad story" voice.

It appeared that I'd been framed and soon I would receive strike three from Eric. I needed to leave—with my Fala chew toy, of course.

But it was gone! I must have released it in the water. And whoever had tried to drown me had taken it away.

"How does it feel to have America watch you slip over the edge on live television?" Laurie asked. She didn't get an answer. I fished my glasses out of the Reflecting Pool and was running once again, this time back to the White House, to find Helen.

26

The Compromise of Helen Thomas

When I got to the White House, I immediately sensed trouble. A fire truck was parked in the driveway. I was already pushing through the turnstile as I flashed my ID to the security guard when he put his hand up.

"Whoa, there, big guy. No one's entering right now."

"What happened? I have to know."

"You and everyone else," he said, motioning with his chin behind me. I turned to see six correspondents already reporting live from Pennsylvania Avenue, the White House as their backdrop. Ordinarily they would have been inside the gate, doing their stand-ups from the lawn.

"Next time wait for a lifeguard before you go for a dip," the guard piped in. I could see that his little TV was turned to Fox News. Apparently he couldn't resist.

From what the correspondents were reporting, something deeply disturbing had happened.

"The explosion seemed to come from somewhere below the lower floor of the pressroom," said Norah O'Donnell to camera.

Before I could imagine the worst, I felt a nipping at my pant leg. I looked down to see not Checkers, but Mr. Peabody looking up at me. So as not to draw attention to himself he was barking like any ordinary dog would. He was even wearing a leash—and holding the leash was Helen! Her eyebrows were singed but she was alive.

"Please, let's go somewhere," she said under her breath. "Quickly."

"THEY'RE CLOSING IN," she said. Helen, Mr. Peabody, and I were sitting in my apartment.

"Someone told them about the archive," she continued. "They might have known about it for a while. It doesn't really matter. They did what I was afraid they'd do—destroyed it and all the evidence of the sacred animal."

It wasn't a simple fire that had been set. The saboteurs dropped a daisy-cutter bomb from above—probably a spare from the war in Afghanistan. The lair was decimated and Helen had barely escaped.

"Thank goodness you were aboveground," she said to Mr. Peabody.

"Yes, thank goodness," he said emphatically. "I just can't imagine how they found out about your archive or why they struck now."

"I'm afraid I might be able to tell you," I said sheepishly. "They have the Fala chew toy."

"What?!" squawked Helen. "But how?"

"It's a long and trippy story," I said. "But I guess now that they have the complete Fala Grail they figured they could destroy the remaining archives, consolidate their power—"

"—and bury the truth forever," said Helen wanly. "Poor Barney is on his own now. If they move against him . . ." She trailed off.

"There, there, Madame," said Mr. Peabody, waxing her new feathers with some shortening I kept in my cupboard. "You can always hope for a miracle, as unlikely as that seems."

"Wait a minute, Helen," I said. "You don't need a miracle. You have your memory—the whole untold history of the White House is in your head. You know the past and if you choose to tell all, then—"

"That's impossible," snapped Mr. Peabody. "Madame cannot divulge such things."

"I still don't understand that," I said. "It makes no sense."

"Mr. Peabody is right," she said. "I can't."

"But why, Helen? The stakes are so high."

Mr. Peabody was becoming more sharp with me than ever before. "It is not for you to know."

"The hell it isn't," I shouted back. "I'm sorry, Mr. Peabody, but it's not just that Bebe Rebozo nearly had me killed. I've been through too much with Helen already to be kept in the dark."

Mr. Peabody raised the canister of shortening over his head, as if he might strike me with it.

But Helen placed her claw on his shoulder. "Mo, I need to level with you," she said. Mr. Peabody begrudgingly backed off.

It was, apparently, time for another confession. Little could shock me at this point. If Helen had somehow unzipped her coat of feathers, revealing the body of a coyote, I would have been bored. Thankfully her revelation was far more interesting.

"I once told you I was never a presidential pet. I'm afraid I was *more* than a presidential pet. As you know, 1848 was a big year for me."

"Actually I didn't know that," I said.

"Well, it was. President Polk was just completing his single extraordinary term. America's territory now stretched coast to coast, thanks to the Mexican-American War, and manifest destiny was reality. That was the year America elected Zachary Taylor president."

"Old Rough and Ready, right? He was a hero of that war."

"That's right. A fearless man. The question was, was he strong enough to deal with the slavery question? Years before I'd been invited to Nat Turner's uprising. It was a lovely affair, before it turned bloody, and the whole experience made me very anti-slavery. I wanted a President who could face down the southern slave interest but Taylor made me uncomfortable. He owned one hundred slaves himself. That's when I met a certain vice president from the state of New York," she said dreamily.

"Millard Fillmore!" I said. "The only President to have no presidential pet."

"You're only half right," she said. "Let me explain. Millard and Abigail Fillmore were delightful. She was a teacher and fervently anti-slavery. And Millard, well, Millard had the most piercing blue eyes you ever saw on a vice president. My God, he made Hannibal Hamlin look like Garret Hobart."

"He was that good-looking?" I asked.

"Hotter than Hubert H. Humphrey," she said, fanning herself with her own wing.

"I got to spending some time with Millard and Abby . . . then just with Millard," she added, lowering her voice and glancing down, a little bit shamefaced. "We got to talking—about my childhood with the Shoshones, his growing up in the Finger Lakes region of New York."

"He built his own house in East Aurora, New York," I chimed in. I'd been there for a tour and purchased a souvenir hot plate.

"Built his own house?" she gaily laughed. "Typical East Aurora hokum. Millard wouldn't have known a hammer if it banged him on his beautiful head." She was clearly still enamored.

She continued. "One evening we got to talking about the congressional deliberations on the Compromise of 1850, a Whig bill meant to stave off war. It had some good provisions—admission of California as a free state and the elimination of slavery in D.C. But Millard seemed worried that President Taylor wouldn't sign it into law."

Helen started pacing around remembering the details of her fateful conversation with the future thirteenth President.

" 'But he's a Whig, too,' I told him. 'Surely he'll side with his party in Congress.'

" 'You silly bird,' he told me. 'Old Rough and Ready's not dealing with a full deck. He's still shell-shocked from the Battle of Buena Vista.' " This was a reference to one of General Taylor's triumphs in the Mexican-American War. " 'So really, there's no telling what Taylor will do about this,' " Helen quoted Fillmore as saying.

"What about Old Whitey?" I asked, referring to Taylor's beloved horse.

"He was a sweet horse," said Helen. "He'd fought with Taylor in Mexico. The trouble was, he lost his hearing, what with all the gunfire. So he was no use to us or him as far as counsel went. Things just felt precarious. That's when Millard made me an offer that I found difficult to refuse. 'I want you to be my presidential pet,' he said. 'Together we can do great things for this country.'

"I was flattered but I figured we'd have to wait until 1856, if President Taylor chose to run for reelection. It was then that I saw Millard look at me as he'd never looked at me before. 'We can't wait that long, Helen,' he said. 'We must act *now*.' "

Helen walked over to the window of my apartment.

"Helen, what are you trying to tell me?" I asked.

Helen was looking out toward the Washington Monument. The cornerstone of the 555-foot obelisk was laid on July 4, 1848. Two years later to the day, President Taylor made his last public appearance at the monument.

"It seems like yesterday," said Helen. "Milk and cherries," she murmured ruefully.

Ice-cold cherries and a pitcher of milk were what Taylor was said to have consumed on that blisteringly hot day in 1850. He dropped dead five days later. The official cause of death was acute indigestion, or gastroenteritis.

I stood and approached Helen. "Milk and cherries. Those *are* what killed Taylor, yes?"

Helen turned to me slowly. "Yes, milk and cherries would kill anyone . . . if they were laced with turkey buzzard E. coli."

I felt as if my heart had stopped. I stumbled back. "No, Helen. No, Helen. No."

"Please listen to me," she said, approaching.

"No, I can't accept it, Helen," I said, turning my head, ashamed.

"Well, you're going to have to accept it." She grabbed my arm, wheeled me around, and looked me straight in the eye. "Yes, Mo. I killed Zachary Taylor. So deal."

I pulled it together. "Helen," I said. "Murder is a very serious crime." It was a pretty stupid statement, but to be fair, I was in shock.

"Yes, Mo, it is. But I was seriously in love. Crazy in love. I believed in Millard—believed that he wanted to make this country a better place for all Americans. After he was sworn in we got right to work. One of the first things we did was prep Commodore Perry for his trip to Japan. Of course there was also time for fun," she added coquettishly. "The first bathtub in the White House had just been installed."

"Uh, Helen, TMI," I cautioned her.

"Right. Well, everything was going along swimmingly until the final proposals of the Compromise of 1850 were presented to President Fillmore. The last one seemed just unimaginable. It was called the Fugitive Slave Act."

The Fugitive Slave Act created a force of commissioners to hunt down runaway slaves, regardless of how long they'd been free, and return them to their owners at ten dollars a head. Citizens who refused to cooperate were fined. It was arguably the most inhumane act of Congress.

Helen continued. " 'You're not going to sign this, Millard,' I said. I actually laughed at the thought, it just seemed so ridiculous. But Millard wasn't laughing. In fact, he stared at me coldly.

" 'You stupid vulture,' he said. 'You really think I'm going to stand up to Congress for some *slaves*?'

" 'But, Millard, you can't. After what I've done for you. I *never* would have pooped in President Taylor's cherry bowl if I thought this would happen. Please don't do this to me. To us!' "

" 'Us?' he snarled. 'You're dumber than a regular turkey.' "

Helen sat down, she was so worked up. Mr. Peabody stood between her and me.

"If you please, my boy, I believe that Madame has upset herself quite enough for today."

"I understand, Helen, and I'm sorry. Fillmore was a bastard to treat you and America's slaves the way that he did. But now you have a chance to come forward and save America's future—so that we don't all become 'slaves.' " It was a stretch, I know, but I was trying to draw a connection. Mr. Peabody rolled his eyes.

"Please, Mo. We've listened to enough of your hectic babbling. If Madame were to speak of what she knows, she would compromise her safety. With all due respect, Madame, you're in no shape to spend a whit of time in a federal penitentiary."

"She won't have to," I snapped.

Helen perked up. "If you've got an idea, what is it?"

I had to think fast, buy some time, before Helen lost heart.

"I'll tell you what you can do: Put on your best dress and get some new shoes. You're my date to the White House Correspondents Dinner."

27

That's Infotainment!

It wasn't much of a plan. But it was the first thing that came to mind. Since 1920 the White House Correspondents Association dinner was one of Washington's most glamorous annual gatherings—luminaries from Washington, New York, and Hollywood dined together. What gave the event its cachet were the quirky guests invited by usually stodgy organizations. The *New York Times* might invite Ozzy Osbourne. Conversely former *Washington Post* editor Ben Bradlee had recently been the guest of *In Style*.

There were few better places to drop a bombshell like Helen's. Everyone who was anyone in media would be there.

But from the moment we entered the Hilton Hotel ballroom it was clear that we were personae non gratae. We expected to be shunned by the White House press corps members. But even those we barely knew gave us the cold shoulder. As we passed by the *National Review* table, Naomi Judd and editor William Buckley whispered about us. The editorial staff of Germany's *Der Spiegel,* seated with David Blaine, were no friendlier. (Blaine had recently wowed the Germans when he scaled the Brandenburg

Gate, removed one of his own kidneys, and swallowed it whole, live on TV.) "Harold *und* Maude," Blaine cackled to his German hosts as he pointed at us.

The one welcoming person was broadcast legend Larry King. He was seated at a table with Phyllis Diller, Carol Channing, and four of Mickey Rooney's ex-wives. They'd just taped a very special episode of *Larry King Live* commemorating the twelfth anniversary of the death of Eve Arden. Next to Larry sat Jane Russell, encased in an iron lung.

Larry welcomed us heartily, but only because he mistook us for the late Martha Raye and her young husband, Mark Harris. Rather than disabuse him of that, we played along.

"How're the dentures workin' out, Martha?" he asked.

"Just fine," Helen said with a grin, confused.

"Well, ya' look like a million bucks!" he said.

On stage Condoleezza Rice was just finishing Rachmaninoff's grueling Etude Tableau in E-flat Minor. Apparently it was a brilliant performance because tears were streaming down Laura Bush's face. "Condi, the music you have played has touched all of our hearts," said the First Lady.

"Thank you, Mrs. Bush," said Condi with a short quick bow. "After dessert I'll be doing an original composition on the French horn—on skates, naturally—per the President's request." She turned on a dime, then marched offstage.

On the dais with the President and Mrs. Bush sat various administration officials and honored guests, as well as Republican comedian Gerald McRaney (TV's Major Dad). He was the only Republican comedian who had yet to perform at one of these events. He rose to address the crowd.

"As a former member of the armed forces," McRaney said cheesily to a smattering of laughter, "I am proud to honor our war President." More applause here. "But now the real show begins. Nothing I say could compare to the entertainment you're about to see. Put your hands together for Hannity and Colmes."

Much to everyone's delight, Hannity and Colmes came out onstage in tramp outfits!

The music started vamping and Hannity and Colmes began swaying to the beat. *We're a couple of swells,* they sang as the audience applauded in recognition.

"Christ, that was a great picture," said Larry King, referring to *Easter Parade.* It was. Naturally Hannity made Colmes take the Judy Garland part, but both of them were terrific.

Helen seemed nervous. "Why are we here, Mo?"

"To tell you the truth, Helen, I don't know exactly. I'm hoping that there's someone here who will listen to your story."

"Well, let's figure it out. I'm not feeling good about this."

Hannity and Colmes were finishing up their number. *Yes, we'll walk up the avenue till we're there!* they sang in conclusion, then scurried offstage as lights came up on a couch. Seated on it were the three hosts of Fox's morning show, *Fox & Friends:* they looked just like Gene Kelly, Donald O'Connor, and Debbie Reynolds.

As the music segued they sprung up from the couch and launched into the "Good Morning" number from *Singin' in the Rain.* By the time the three ended up back on the couch laughing and falling backward, the crowd was going crazy. I could even hear Jane Russell applauding from inside her casing.

Then the lights faded to black and the audience fell silent.

"What's happening?" whispered Helen anxiously. David Gest (the former Mr. Liza Minnelli and a guest of the *New England Journal of Medicine*) shushed her.

Center stage a single spotlight had come up on Fox News contributor Mara Liasson, dangerously sexy in a black satin sheath dress. She leaned against an upright piano played by fellow contributor Juan Williams. Curls of smoke rose from below as she began crooning her ten o'clock number:

> *Oh Mr. Ailes, I love him so*
> *He'll never know*

All my life I sang the blues
Then came Fox News

It was clear that, like Fanny Brice, Mara was not simply a comedienne. She was also a brilliant chanteuse.

Now I'm a cable TV star
So it's so long to N . . . P . . . R . . .

The way she held and caressed the "R" in "NPR" made everyone feel as if she were singing to him or her alone—the mark of a great performer. Mara was heartbreakingly good.

The spotlight faded on her again and the music swelled as a voice-over announced, "Ladies and gentlemen, please welcome Roger Ailes and the fairest, most balanced starlets in the entire cable news universe!"

From stage left and right, a line of Fox starlets, each in identical gold lamé leotards and platinum blond wigs, came tap dancing out, Busby Berkeley style. The mournful jazz piano was replaced by a rollicking big band that slid in on a platform upstage right, as the girls sang along uptempo:

What's ailing you?
Red White and Blue
No need to feel so lonely!

What's ailing you?
Come on, be true
Fox News is here for you only!

The tune was infectious and the girls were gorgeous. And then there were the guys. A line of movie-star-handsome Fox News men in matching gold tuxedos came tapping out and paired off with the girls. Shepard Smith and Judith Regan made the most dazzling pair.

"They're cookin' with gas!" said Larry King, slapping his hands together. The dancers were perfectly in sync, pausing only for a wailing cornet solo by *Weekly Standard* editor Fred Barnes. That's when dance soloist Morton Kondracke started doing "wings," always a crowd-pleaser. When all the dancers joined back in, the glass ceiling tilted forward so that the audience could see the reflection as the dancers came together in a pinwheel, before spreading out to spell "News Corp." President Bush was slack-jawed, a kid in a candy store.

The number was approaching a climax as everyone on stage parted in the center and a giant Lucite staircase rolled forward from the back of the stage. The dancers all gestured toward the top and sang:

> *Hey look up there*
> *Balanced and fair*
> *Here come the pair of the hour!*

With a cymbal crash all the music stopped. The dancers were frozen and we were all on the edges of our seats. We knew what was coming but a subtle drum roll still built suspense.

Then it happened. Appearing at the top of the staircase were Laurie Dhue and Roger Ailes—Laurie in a radiant gown, Mr. Ailes in top hat, tails, and a cane. The music resumed more lushly than before as the dancers "aah"-ed in harmony and a beautifully lit fountain of water began gushing downstage.

As Laurie and Mr. Ailes descended, each step they touched lit up. When they got to the bottom, Laurie turned to Mr. Ailes and in a voice as warm as Doris Day's sang out:

> *Hey there, hey you*
> *I'm Laurie Dhue*
> *There is no need to be lonely*

Typical promo for Fox News.

Mr. Ailes smiled. Laurie continued:

> *Don't you be blue*
> *I'm here for you*
> *I'm here for Mr. Ailes only*

It was a thrilling moment as Laurie tore off her gown—she wore a sequined body stocking underneath—and went into her fiery, some might say manic, Ann Miller dance. Much to my surprise, Helen was less interested in the show.

"I've had enough," she snapped, getting up from the table and marching into the hallway.

"The good ones always get away," said Larry King to me in his guy-to-guy voice, looking after Helen. I chased after her, right into the ladies' bathroom.

"Helen, what's wrong?" I said.

"I can't do this. No one will believe what I have to say. It's too late anyway."

"What do mean 'too late'?"

"Come on, Mo. They say Barney has rickets. Even if the President loves him, the press office has probably already finished him off."

"But you can still talk, Helen. To someone, anyone."

"Why would someone believe a presidential assassin?" she asked.

Before I could make up an answer, the door flew open. Former UN ambassador Jeane Kirkpatrick and teen sensation Mandy Moore rushed in and frantically started primping in the mirror.

"What's going on?" I asked. They were so excited they didn't even ask why I was in the ladies' room.

"Barney's here!" squealed Mandy.

"And we're getting our pictures taken with him!" shrieked

Ambassador Kirkpatrick. The two girls ran out as quickly as they'd come in.

"He's here," said Helen. "That means . . ."

". . . we can talk to him directly," I said. "Helen, this may be our one and only chance."

"Right on," said Helen with surging confidence. "We've got to talk to Barney."

Helen and I headed toward the bathroom exit when one of the stall doors swung open, blocking us.

"Watch it!" I said, before I was looking down the barrel of a gun. Standing at the entrance to the stall, holding a gun in his black gloved paw, was none other than Mr. Peabody.

"Mr. Peabody, what are you doing!" I asked.

"I'm detaining you—*permanently,*" he said. This wasn't a joke.

"But I don't understand," said Helen.

"No, you don't, Madame," sighed Mr. Peabody. "You really don't. I tried to spare you this fate. I wanted to let you die a natural death. Killing isn't one of my favorite pastimes. Really it isn't. But sadly you had to persist."

"Mr. Peabody, you can harm me but you can't—" I began.

"For once in your life, shut up!" he snapped, then turned back to Helen. "I let you bring your little boy-toy in on your secret. I assumed that once you passed, he would continue flailing about on basic cable. If he ever tried to tell all he knew, he'd never be believed. But then you got a little too serious. And you made the big mistake of giving him the Fala chew toy."

"So you're the one who grabbed the chew toy?" I asked.

"Come now," said Mr. Peabody. "Even I'm not that pale."

It was Gephardt the Albino who'd grabbed it. And Mr. Peabody was the short figure in the cowl. It was all coming together now.

Mr. Peabody continued. "And now you've come here. Your *final* mistake."

I had to speak up. "Mr. Peabody, the First Dog is right out there and he won't be silenced by people like you."

"You fool," Mr. Peabody laughed. "First of all, I'm a dog. Secondly, I'll soon be the *First Dog!*"

Helen shook her head, uncomprehending. "But why, Tad? You had such a promising career in academia."

"Publish or perish," Mr. Peabody snarled bitterly. "Without an offer of tenure I was screwed. But soon I'll have more clout than any pissant liberal arts department chair in America."

"You'll never pull this off," I said.

"I won't, will I?" he laughed. "You don't think I can become a national icon? I can't bark like a First Dog?" He barked. "I can't beg up?" He begged up. "I can't slobber?" He slobbered. "I can't roll over?" He rolled over. "I can't be adorable?" He posed, sort of adorably, I have to admit. "I can't frolic, you say?" He started frolicking and laughing at the two of us. "See there, I'm frolicking! Tad Peabody is frolicking!!"

Mr. Peabody was so into his frolic, gun in paw swinging about, that I saw my chance. With both hands I grabbed his paw, right below the gun. (That area of the dog is actually called the pastern.) There was a struggle. He was stronger than I thought.

"Put the gun . . . down, Peabody." Peabody's hand was trembling as he tried desperately to steer the gun toward my face.

With all the strength I could muster I squeezed his wrist until he dropped the gun. In a flash Helen reached under her dress and pulled out her girdle. With some lightning-fast scoutmaster knots she used it to bind and gag Peabody inside one of the stalls.

"Let's go," said Helen.

We reentered the ballroom just as Laurie and Mr. Ailes were completing the eighteen-minute closing ballet sequence from *An American in Paris.*

There up on the dais was Barney nuzzling against President

Bush's leg. From across the crowded room, our eyes met. As Laurie leaped into Mr. Ailes's arms at the end of the dance, the audience rose to its feet with ecstatic applause. It was perfect timing.

I began moving toward Barney, my eyes locked with his, through the still standing and applauding crowd. I was on a different plane, sailing toward Barney in a straight line, Helen right by my side.

The first suspicious look I noticed was Paul Wolfowitz. He signaled to communications director Dan Bartlett, who threw a signal to Scott McClellan. Scott shot a look to Gephardt the Albino, who from the far side of the room started approaching. Gephardt was closing in as Helen and I quickened our pace toward Barney. Would he manage to cut us off? That was anyone's guess.

Then, as luck should have it, Gephardt got stalled behind the *Washington Post*'s Sally Quinn, who was engrossed in a conversation with *Full House*'s John Stamos. The way to Barney looked clear until Gephardt, in a sudden fit of pique, struck Stamos against the head. A cry went up as Jane Seymour, the former Dr. Quinn, Medicine Woman, knelt down to examine him.

Gephardt the Albino was now racing toward us, so Helen and I did the same toward Barney. We were mere feet away when from out of nowhere Laurie, a look of distress behind her wide smile, stepped in front of us with two armed guards. Straining to sound casual she said, "Well, how lovely to see you both. Now let these gentlemen escort you *out . . .* before all hell breaks loose." The two guards grabbed us and started pushing us out.

I looked over my shoulder, straining to keep eye contact with Barney, our last best hope. He looked back at me wanly. "Goodbye and God bless America," I said feebly. We both understood she would need our prayers.

But Helen wasn't going so gently.

"Ouch!" yelled one of the armed guards. In a flash Helen had bitten his arm and scurried between his legs. She was running toward Barney. Helen was going to make contact.

The guard looked helpless. The President looked confused. But Laurie stood between Helen and Barney.

And Laurie looked pissed.

28

The Chapter That
Only Jerry Bruckheimer
Could Bring to Film

Fixing her with a terrifying stare, Laurie suddenly thrust out her hand toward Helen. Helen backed up, but Laurie's arm instantly extended and her hand gripped Helen's skull. Helen squawked.

"Uh-oh, looks like trouble," said the President, grabbing Mrs. Bush and Barney and diving under the table. The rest of the dais followed.

I slipped past my guard and tried to wrest Laurie's grip from Helen's head but when I touched her arm I felt cold steel. Then when I picked up a chair to crash over her, her head pivoted toward me at an impossible angle and her neck literally extended in a serpentine flash. She gripped the chair with her teeth, smashing it over my head.

"Oh my God," screamed ABC's Kate Snow. "Laurie Dhue is a cyborg!"

That's when it occurred to me. "Daresay Glib Curio," I said, dazed. "That's an anagram for 'Laurie D. is a cyborg' . . . wow, what a stupid anagram." I had barely hobbled to my feet when Gephardt the Albino's black shiny military boot kicked me in the face. I fell backward. Luckily former press secretary Marlin Fitzwater was there to break my fall. Gephardt was determined to silence me for good, though. He picked me up off Fitzwater and hurled me right at *Laugh-In*'s Jo Anne Worley. I managed to pull myself together and take a swing at Gephardt. He caught my hand and began crushing it.

Then out of nowhere, Wolf flew in and pointed a flashpoint at Gephardt. Gephardt howled in pain. "Albinos suffer from photophobia," I remembered. "Great thinking, Wolf!" Then with a flying roundhouse kick to the head, Wolf managed to knock Gephardt out cold.

"Oh my God, Wolf Blitzer is a black belt!" exclaimed Kate Snow.

"Wolf-san, thank you," I said, but there was little time for chitchat. Laurie's grip was tightening on Helen's head. Helen projectile-vomited, the common reaction for a buzzard when cornered, but Laurie didn't blink.

Wolf went for broke and leaped at Laurie with the same move that had knocked out Gephardt. This time Laurie's free hand morphed into a giant flyswatter and with the power of two hundred Williams sisters combined, smacked Wolf into the ceiling, where he stuck flat for a moment before dropping onto a chandelier. He hung there unconscious.

Laurie was using her hand-turned-flyswatter to bat aside anyone who approached. When a courageous George Stephanopolous charged toward her, Laurie's flyswatter morphed into a bat. Like a champion slugger she pointed her bat across the room toward Ali Wentworth, then line-drived George right into his wife.

"Good to see you two 'livin' it up'!" Laurie growled in a deep demonic voice.

All looked lost till Candy stepped up. From out of her overstuffed purse, she pulled her pearl-handled revolver. Candy aimed right at Laurie's midsection, closed her eyes tight, and fired. With a loud ping sound, the bullet ricocheted off Laurie's titanium torso and right into Dr. Phil's ass. Like a barnyard animal he wailed in pain.

Laurie was laughing, her eyes bright red. She was channeling James Earl Jones now. "Something tells me that you *can't* depend on CNN."

Candy was undaunted. "I'll report—and I'll decide. Bitch." Candy gave her purse a few good swings, then walloped Laurie in the head. A loud crunching sound was heard and Laurie fell backward, releasing Helen.

"Candy, you're amazing!" I shouted.

"They don't call me 'Handy Candy' for nothin'," she said, opening her purse and pouring out the dust of a couple of shattered Hummel figurines. "I knew these things were worth something."

Helen was getting her breath back. "I'll be fine, dear. But I don't think we're through with her," she said, pointing to the spot on the floor where Laurie had fallen. There was now a metallic liquid pool and within seconds it was quickly re-forming itself into a human shape.

With Laurie regenerating herself, Helen did the only sensible thing: she flew upward to safety.

"Haven't done this in years," she said. With a few flaps she was soaring up above.

"Oh my God!" said Kate Snow, "Helen Thomas is a bald eagle!"

"That's not an eagle, you dingbat," snapped Norah O'Donnell. "It's a turkey buzzard."

The reporters were now furiously taking notes, their attention on Helen making lazy circles in the sky. She was absolutely beautiful in flight, her wings spread in a spectacular dihedral V-formation.

"Helen," I said, my voice catching, "you're beautiful."

Back down on the ground, though, danger reemerged. A liquid metal Laurie Dhue strode up onto the stage. Once transmogrified back into flesh she was wearing a pink prom dress and looking suspiciously like Sissy Spacek in *Carrie*. That's when, as promised, all hell broke loose. First all the doors slammed shut, then a fire hose started gushing on its own.

"Jesus Christ," I murmured. "Laurie Dhue has telekinetic powers."

The cannon-strength water jet immediately took out three of Mickey Rooney's ex-wives. Larry King was smart enough to hide behind Jane Russell's iron lung. The hose next went after defense attorney Mark Geragos and pinned him against the wall. In a touching moment, his nemesis, Court TV's Nancy Grace, pulled him to safety only to be blown through a window herself.

Suddenly an I beam dropped down, collapsing on Dick Morris's feet. Above the chaos you could hear the crunching of Dick's delicate foot bones. "My feeeeeeeeee—!" he screamed.

A sinkhole opened up in the floor and in a moment straight out of *Earthquake* Barbara Boxer and Joe Biden—the Senate's closest likenesses to Ava Gardner and Charlton Heston—were whisked away.

The horrific chaos instantly brought some people closer together. Former senator Alan Simpson grabbed NPR's Nina Totenberg, soaked but ravishing, and they began furiously making out—before they were engulfed in flames.

As a measure of how things had gotten out of hand, Ann Coulter looked at Laurie, then turned to me: "Okay, I think she's overreacting." That was seconds before Secretary of Energy Spencer Abraham dropped on top of her.

I knew I didn't want to die this way so I sought shelter in a remarkably sturdy barricade that Condoleezza Rice had thrown together from a couple of tables and chairs. Inside Condi was working three cell phones while she loaded a shoulder-fired missile.

"The President believes that what is going on in the Hilton Hotel is unacceptable to the American people. The President recognizes, however, that Laurie Dhue is not representative of the many honest, decent, patriotic cyborgs that are a welcome, vibrant part of American society," she shouted into the phone. When MSNBC Joe Scarborough's head rolled behind the barricade, Condi gave it a curious look, then set it on fire and hurled it Molotov cocktail–style back at Laurie, all without missing a beat. While Condi continued spinning I peered over the barricade, in search of Helen.

Smoke and water were filling the room quickly and the cries of the press corps, politicians, and assorted quirky personalities were agonizing to hear.

Across the room I could see that Candy was stranded on top of a table, the water rising around her. She took a deep breath, then swan-dived in and swam underwater. When she came up, coughing and spitting up water, she dragged John King in one arm and a surprisingly unironic Leslie Nielsen in the other.

Meanwhile Alan Colmes had become hysterical. All dressed up for the "Waiters' Gallop" number from *Hello, Dolly!* he stood in front of Laurie ranting. "What have you done with Hannity?!" he shrieked.

Surely Laurie was about to do something unspeakable to him but she suddenly had other priorities. Pushing me aside from behind, Condi had stepped forward. And this sister meant business. She fired her missile right into the wall next to Laurie. The water drained out and suddenly there was a glimmer of hope for the living. Next Condi pulled a lump of coal from out of her pocket, then crushed it in her fist so hard that when she opened her hand there was a diamond there—all just to show how bad-ass she was. She tossed it carelessly over her shoulder. (Like a lizard snapping at a mosquito, a maimed David Gest snatched it.)

Laurie was impressed. The two eyed each other with cool suspicion as Condi drew nearer. It looked like Condi just might save us, but we were still on edge.

"You're gonna kill us all!" screamed an unhinged Ernest Borgnine. Condi knocked him out with the back of her hand.

"She's going to need enforcements," said General Eric Shinseki, shaking his head.

"Keep it lean, keep it mean, Condi," countered Donald Rumsfeld.

"You break it, you fix it," piped in Colin Powell. "Pottery Barn rules."

"Pardon me, Secretary, but that's not Pottery Barn policy," corrected Pottery Barn CEO Howard Lester from underneath Donald Trump's lifeless body.

Condi heard nothing. She'd come face to face with Laurie. The moment was at hand.

The smallest of smiles played across Laurie's face as a pair of wraparound sunglasses morphed onto her face and a trenchcoat onto her body. Condi, not to be outdone, snapped her fingers, and Paul Wolfowitz threw her an identical ensemble.

Condi leaped into the air and hung there, it seemed, in slow motion, arms outstretched, until one leg snapped forward and connected with Laurie's chin. Then everything lurched back into real time as Condi pummeled her so furiously her hands were a blur.

"It's a slam dunk!" shouted former CIA chief George Tenet, jumping up and down and waving his arms.

But Laurie regained her footing and bolted away from Condi, actually running up and along the wall, executing a perfect double back flip and straddling Condi from behind. Condi grabbed for the nearest weapon, UN Secretary-General Kofi Annan, and began mercilessly thrashing him against Laurie—but to no avail. Crushed in the vise-like grip of Laurie's thighs, Condi began sputtering, her fluent bureaucratese now faltering: "In the context of the offending structural impediment only one actionable conclusion can be ascertained . . . Richard Clarke . . . is one major . . . mofo," before quietly surrendering.

Laurie, her eyes flickering with an eerie calm, would now likely finish the rest of us off.

"Where the hell are you, Helen?" I said.

Then up above from out of the smoke Helen came soaring. She was still alive! And she was heading straight toward Wolf, who was still knocked out, sprawled inside the chandelier—which just happened to hang directly over Laurie, who was continuing to wage her campaign of terror.

It was immediately clear what Helen was trying to do. She started pecking away at the cable connecting the chandelier to the ceiling. Wolf was coming to when Helen gnawed the very last connective tendril of cable.

Laurie had just sent a set of steak knives flying toward Chris Matthews when the chandelier came loose. She looked up but didn't have a second to stop the chandelier from crashing down on her.

Helen swooped down and pulled out Wolf before the sound of a massive electrocution started. Laurie was sparking and smoking like a trunk of firecrackers set on fire. It was a spectacular short-circuiting as Laurie's systems went totally haywire:

"Fair and balanced . . . Welcome to *The Dig Story* . . . fair and balanced . . . stay tuned for *The O'Reilly Factor* . . . I'm Laurie Dhue . . . More news at the bottom of the hour . . . the network that America trusts . . . let's turn it over to Oliver North . . ."

Then it stopped. The violence was over.

Only the cries of the injured and dying continued—along to the sweet strains of Mandy Moore's spontaneous cover of "There's Got to Be a Morning After."

CNN's Dr. Sanjay Gupta was doing all he could to minister to the wounded. (Those at the *Christian Science Monitor* table politely refused treatment.)

"—eeeeeeeeeeeet," finished screaming Dick Morris. Out of breath, he simply whimpered.

His bald head beaded with sweat, James Carville just muttered. "The horror. The horror."

I hobbled to Helen's side. "Are you okay, Helen?"

"Don't worry about me, darling," she said, choking on the

fumes. "What happened to Barney?" The dais was shrouded in smoke. For all we knew there were no survivors up there. The podium was only barely visible.

Then like the American flag at Fort McHenry, one tiny paw reached up from behind it. Then another. Then small though it was, the head of a proud Scottie rose up and began speaking into the microphone, which was miraculously still working!

"I speak to you tonight, not as a Republican, not as a Democrat, but as a Pet," he began resonantly, with only the slightest hint of his ancestors' burr. "A Presidential Pet who was proud to answer the call to serve his great country, a country founded on the wisdom of the pets who came before. But sadly, I have not been able to serve my country . . ."

My heart was racing and I put my arm around Helen. This was the moment we'd all been waiting for. Barney continued:

"The astonishing tale I will tell is one that I hope will inspire a new birth of freedom." He paused. "But damn if I'm going to tell it for free to a room full of dead people. ICM, if you're out there, you know where to call."

Barney padded off stage, chased after by a limping Ron Suskind waving a blackened business card.

Once again the room fell eerily silent, until the double doors flew open and a young woman in an Eskimo coat and Ugg boots strode in and dropped her suitcases. "Am I late?" chirped Ashleigh Banfield, all smiles before taking in the devastation before her.

29

In Which Everything Ends Happily for Everyone Except the Several Dozen Casualties in Chapter 28

Needless to say, the carnage at the Hilton was replayed ad nauseam. In the end, everyone won out.

CNN and MSNBC both saw big spikes in their ratings. More important, their reporters were reenergized after learning all they'd been missing. They stood together and forced the administration to become much more open—no more background briefings, no more ignoring reporters' phone calls, no more dropping bad news on Friday in the hopes it wouldn't get coverage, no more threats against Barney.

President Bush, it turned out, was unharmed. Seconds after the melee had begun, he'd been whisked off to a bunker in Nebraska. Later, when he heard about Barney speaking, he was genuinely surprised. "All those times I heard that voice, I thought it was Jesus talkin' to me." He vowed to make both himself and Barney available for regular press conferences—so long as they could appear jointly and he be allowed to continue using stupid nicknames for reporters.

The secret note in the press secretary's vest, it turned out, had the message "Muzzle him" written on it, presumably in reference to the First Pet—fairly uninspired in comparison with everything else that had gone on. Scott was only too happy to be rid of Gephardt the Albino. "He kind of freaked me out," he admitted.

Eric Sorenson got promoted to NBC's executive offices and immediately offered me my own show. I demurred, choosing to take some time out to recover from the wound left by a salad fork driven into my side. (After a quick rehab and a few simple skin grafts, Joe Scarborough took the slot.)

One interesting byproduct: Ashleigh Banfield got rehired by NBC. The network was now severely understaffed so her timing had been perfect.

Fox News, already the cable news ratings leader, saw the biggest boost in their numbers. Laurie's display of telekinetic pyrotechnic terror was all caught on tape and repeated more than the Howard Dean scream speech. Suddenly the coveted young male viewers who'd mysteriously stopped watching television the season before returned en masse to Fox News. "She's hot and she kills people," explained one teen.

At great expense the network chose to rebuild Laurie. It was worth every penny. In the meantime they used a sample of her cyborg DNA to clone a more modestly lipped duplicate, code name Paige Hopkins.

As for Helen, her fears of going to jail for the murder of Zachary Taylor proved unfounded. Legal analyst Jeffrey Toobin, another Hilton massacre survivor, informed her that the statute of limitations on the murder of that President had already passed.

Helen was a free woman and the toast of the town. She received a Peabody, a Polk, a People's Choice, and she got to host *TRL*.

But the greatest honor was the one bestowed by the Turkey Vulture Society. We arrived at their awards ceremony in the new stretch Prius. I held Helen's claw as her name was called. When Helen made her way onto the stage, she was overwhelmed.

"This moment is so much bigger than me. This is for Dorothy Dandridge, Lena Horne, and the California condor," she said, waving her statuette. "A door has been opened!"

She was the most sought after interview—or "get"—of the season. Every one of broadcast television's biggest names went after Helen with an appalling relentlessness.

The most extravagant offer was made by CBS, a division of Viacom. The package included a sit-down with *60 Minutes*'s Ed Bradley, a guest spot on *CSI: Miami,* a sitcom pilot on UPN, a roast on Comedy Central, a Jacob watch from BET, a book deal from Simon & Schuster, and a suitcase packed with five million dollars in unmarked bills (through CBS's entertainment division, of course). The offer was tempting but the added perk of an MTV concert in her hometown featuring the rock group the Cranberries was just insulting.

"They think I'm a turkey!" said Helen, disgusted.

ABC's Diane Sawyer made the same mistake: She sent Helen three bags of grain and an offer to do an interview on Plimouth Plantation. Helen accepted this offer, though.

"Diane used to leak me all sorts of information during the Nixon administration. I've got a soft spot for her," she explained.

Helen insisted I go with her for the interview. Diane, Helen, and I nestled together on an L-shaped haystack. But Diane, outfitted in overalls, only wanted to talk about Helen's relationship with Millard Fillmore.

"Here you were, a turkey buzzard no older than fifty and in *love* with the vice president," Diane said with extra breathiness.

"It wasn't easy, Diane," Helen sighed. "I was just so young." She was better at this than I thought she'd be.

Diane paused meaningfully. "If you had to do it all again, Helen, would you?"

"Every last minute, Diane," she said, then remembered to add, "well, maybe not the murdering the President part."

(Helen's sit-down with Charlie Rose was less successful. By the time Charlie finished asking his first question, the hour was up.)

The next big decision involved choosing who would do the authorized television documentary of Helen's life. Because I'd worked with Harry Smith I put in a word for A&E's *Biography*. But Ken Burns made the most impassioned pitch for a 352-hour film about her life. "We won't actually need to interview you. Just give us a few snapshots to pan over and Linda Hunt will lay down the voice-overs."

Helen rejected both in favor of Truman biographer and PBS host David McCullough. "Talk about a hot piece of ass!" she exclaimed when his name came up.

Helen spent hours touching up her crop before their meeting. David proposed a ten-hour special profile of Helen for PBS's *American Experience*. She said yes to every idea he suggested, not that she heard a word of what he said.

"Helen, you do realize that he's married?"

"Married. Not dead," she snapped.

Of course not everything panned out. The *Hollywood Reporter* trumpeted the long-awaited return of the variety show after Animal Planet offered one to Helen. They agreed to give her a stage with a giant "HELEN" written out in lights. Helen walked away from the offer, though, when the network insisted she work with a sidekick salamander voiced over by Jerry Van Dyke.

As for the writing of Helen's story, I decided to go ahead and give it a shot, but Ken Auletta beat me to the punch with a 430,000-word piece for *The New Yorker* (still shorter than his profile of Harvey Weinstein). Then Tom Brokaw came out with his own book, at which point Tom Hanks and Bob Dole jumped onto the bandwagon with a proposal for a Presidential Pets Memorial.

The design competition was fierce. In the end Maya Lin's brooding dog bowl sunk into the ground was rejected as too much of a downer. Instead the committee designed their own monument: a 750-foot-tall alabaster bone that completely overshadowed the Washington Monument. (D.C.'s height restriction was waived.) To help defray the cost, Iams, the major sponsor, had its name etched along the side. It was all pretty obscene, but no one wanted to go

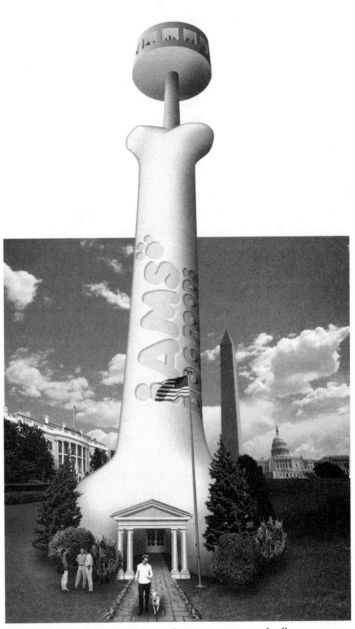

The Presidential Pet Memorial, Washington's newest and tallest monument.

against the mood. And to be fair, even L'Enfant would've admitted that the observation deck was pretty cool.

Barney ended up not writing his own book. Instead he felt mysteriously compelled to tell all to reporter Bob Woodward. Woodward's book, clunkily titled *All the Presidents' Animals,* was delayed due to the sheer number of other insider pets who'd lined up to confess their every secret to him. Early word had it that the book chronicled a nasty breakdown in communication between Colin Powell's tabby cat and Dick Cheney's cobra.

Mr. Peabody wrote his own book. *Burning Down My Master's Doghouse* was heavily promoted but never broke #2,000 on Amazon's sales ranking. He tried to return to the time machine business but despite Lou Dobbs's best efforts, his job got outsourced.

THAT DECEMBER I ESCORTED Helen to the White House Christmas party.

I knew that my stock had risen when early in the evening, Kate Snow and Norah O'Donnell, wearing brand-new Pink Ladies jackets, approached me and invited me to take part in their spring-break Cancún house.

"It's going to be a blast!" said Kate.

"Hello-o?" said Norah. "It's going to be a *major* blast."

"Wow," I said. "That's really nice of you. I'd love to but I already promised Candy and Jim Angle that I'd go to Atlantic City with them . . . Sorry." I dreaded the prospect of becoming unpopular again.

But Norah and Kate were still smiling. "If you change your mind, just call," Norah said.

Just then the United States Marine Band—dubbed "The President's Own" by Jefferson—struck up a medley of Bee Gees songs. The *Washington Post*'s Dana Milbank rushed in excitedly. "Helen and Mo, we're waiting!"

Helen and I, happy at last.

It was 1985 again but instead of Princess Diana and John Travolta wowing everyone with their dancing at the Reagan White House, Helen and I were doing a mean hustle in the East Room.

The room was spinning in one direction as Helen and I turned in the other. Laura Bush and Barney looked on, beaming. President Bush clapped his hands to the beat, sort of. But when the dance ended, Helen seemed unusually winded.

She whispered in my ear: "I don't feel well."

30

All the Presidents' Pets

THE NEXT GENERATION

I didn't see Helen for three weeks. We spoke only occasionally, but she wasn't her chatty self. She sounded so tired and weighed down.

Finally one day she called me with news. "Something has happened. I want you to come over."

The Army Corps of Engineers had agreed to rebuild Helen's lair after its destruction. Until then Helen was living in a quaint apartment in Woodley Park, just across from the zoo. I rushed over to see her.

A somber Jack Hanna, in a lab coat and stethoscope, answered the door. "Hello, I'm Helen's nurse," he said.

"Nurse?! I'm here to see Helen," I said. "Is she okay?" I was led into a small, sunny room. Helen was crouched down in a corner. She looked exhausted.

"Mo," she said faintly. "You've come."

"Yes, Helen, how could I stay away? I've been worried sick. Now I see you're receiving medical care. What's wrong?"

Helen said nothing. She simply stood up, revealing two large eggs she'd been sitting on. The eggs were cream-colored, splashed toward the larger end with irregular markings of brown and black, approximately $2\frac{7}{8}$ inches in length.

"Helen! You're going to have babies."

"Yes, I am," she smiled wanly. "But I have something else to tell you. I'm not going to be returning to the White House."

"What?!"

"I'm done for. My days in the press corps are over," she said stoically. "I'm . . . moving on."

I was immediately overcome. I threw myself on the floor in front of her, my body racked by sobs. "Helen, you're my true friend. I can't just let you die! Please, Helen, I need you," I heaved.

"Pull yourself together," snapped Helen. "I'm sticking around until at least the 2036 election—the smart money's on George P."

"Oh, Helen," I said, wiping the tears from my eyes.

Just then a cracking sound was heard from Helen's nest. The eggs were hatching! The babies were miniature Helens, except that their bills were tipped with pale blue and their irises more yellowish, typical for newborn buzzards. Each of them held little steno pads. They were ready for work.

"Salutations!" they chirped in unison.

"Aren't they just adorable?" beamed Helen.

"Adorable? What's 'adorable'?" they asked in unison. "We're hungry." Helen lovingly regurgitated some hedgehog carrion and gave her girls their first feeding.

"Yummy! Thank you, Mommy!" they sang, then frowned at Helen. "But you didn't answer the question," they scowled. "What's 'adorable'?"

"Oh, here we go," said Helen. "Listen, Mo, I hate to be rude but I've got my hands full right now. The girls won't be ready for the White House beat till they're full grown."

"That's seventy to eighty days," I said.

"Right. Until then I've got lots to teach them. Ugh, I just know I'm never going to be able to see a movie again!"

"I'll get you a subscription to Netflix. Anyway, I'll let you go, Helen." Most of my friends with newborns were so busy I knew it would be a long time before I'd see her again. "Thanks again for everything, Helen. You've changed my life."

"Well, you've certainly changed mine," she responded flatly, with a look toward her chicks.

I had been lucky: It is not often that someone comes along who is a true friend and a good reporter. Helen was both.

AFTER I HELPED HER install her car seats, I left and walked down to the Mall, to the Presidential Pet Memorial. I was in a meditative mood.

Climbing the steps, I thought of the greatness that had shaped our country. The nobility of Washington's horse Nelson. The conviction of Kennedy's dogs Charlie and Pushinka. The courage of Grant's gamecocks. (They're in the sequel.)

As I stepped out on the observation deck I was so high I could see the Potomac River and the Chesapeake Bay beyond, and ever so faintly in the distance the Atlantic Ocean, upon which Reverend Winthrop once sermonized about "a City upon a Hill." Damn, this thing is tall.

Perhaps Barney could one day join that pantheon of the great presidential pets who had helped make America a beacon. With the vigilance of me and the rest of the press corps, he stood a chance.

The Presidents and Their Pets

A SELECTED LIST

GEORGE WASHINGTON

Washington deserves the additional moniker "Father of the American foxhound" after crossing General Lafayette's gift of seven stag hounds—among them, **Sweet Lips, Scentwell,** and **Vulcan**—with his own smaller black-and-tan Virginia hounds—among them **Drunkard, Taster, Tipler,** and **Tipsy**—to create "a superior dog, one that had speed, scent, and brains."

Royal Gift the jackass did indeed sire a race of "supermules."

Nelson the horse carried Washington to Cornwallis's surrender at Yorktown.

JOHN ADAMS

Dogs **Juno** and **Satan** offered the man known as the "Duke of Braintree" solace after his humiliating loss in the election of 1800.*

The presidential stables were built for his favorite horse, **Cleopatra.**

---

* Adams's bulldog Toddy (Chapter 11) is one of only two fictionalized pets in this book. I needed a male dog for the Crossfire debate, and using Satan would have seemed a little too editorial.

THOMAS JEFFERSON

Buzzy the Briard sheepdog sailed back from France with the president.

Several unnamed grizzly bears, a gift from either Lewis and Clark or Lt. Zebulon Pike, were caged on the White House lawn, which political opponents soon dubbed "The President's Bear Garden."

Dick the mockingbird was a constant companion.

(Jefferson once said that maintaining slavery was like "holding a wolf by the ears." There is no record of his ever having had wolves.)

JAMES MADISON

First Lady Dolley saved three things when the British burned down the White House in 1814: the portrait of George Washington, the Declaration of Independence, and **Polly** the Parrot. The President had fled hours before.

JAMES MONROE

Monroe's daughter Hester Maria had a black spaniel, name unknown.

JOHN QUINCY ADAMS

President Adams and his wife, Louisa, reared silkworms.

An alligator brought by the Marquis de Lafayette during an 1825 visit resided in the East Room for several months.

ANDREW JACKSON

Old Hickory's obscene parrot **Pol** was found in a Nashville confectioner's shop.

His prized Tennessee fighting cocks all suffered defeat against Virginia fighting cocks.

MARTIN VAN BUREN

The "Little Magician" was forced by Congress to give his two tiger cubs, a gift from Kabul al Said, Sultan of Oman, to the zoo.

(Van Buren was vilified for allowing the War Department to use Cuban bloodhounds to remove Seminoles from Florida in 1840 and track down runaway slaves.)

WILLIAM HENRY HARRISON

Sukey the cow was purchased locally and barely had time to get to know her president.

JOHN TYLER

Le Beau the Italian greyhound was sent from Naples.

Johnny Ty the canary was single until President Tyler found him a mate. But after the mate was added to the cage, Johnny died within a week. The mate turned out to be male!

Tyler wrote the following epitaph for his horse **The General**: "For years he bore me around the circuit of my practice and all that time he never made a blunder. Would that his master could say the same . . ."

JAMES K. POLK

He had a horse.

ZACHARY TAYLOR

Old Whitey the horse was knock-kneed and as misshapen as his President. Visitors plucked souvenir hairs from his tail.

MILLARD FILLMORE

No pets, at least *officially*.

FRANKLIN PIERCE

President Pierce received seven miniature Oriental dogs and two birds from Japan, part of a large consignment marking the opening of diplomatic relations. He gave one of the birds to Mrs. Jefferson Davis, though he probably never remembered doing so, since he was *never sober.*

JAMES BUCHANAN

Lara the 170-pound Newfoundland became a celebrity, known for lying motionless for hours at a time with one eye open.

Punch the tiny toy terrier was a gift from the U.S. consul in South Hampton, England.

The King of Siam sent along a herd of elephants.

Two bald eagles were a gift from a "friend" in San Francisco.

ABRAHAM LINCOLN

Lincoln indulged his boys, Tad and Willie, with a menagerie of animals, including two ponies. Not long after Willie's death, the two ponies were trapped in a fire, from which the president unsuccessfully tried to rescue them.

Tad found contentment with his goats, **Nanny** and **Nanko.**

Jack the turkey was originally slated for Christmas dinner. The sentence was reprieved after Tad's plea for clemency.

Fido the mongrel was the first presidential pet to be photographed. He followed Lincoln's funeral procession throughout Springfield. A year later he was stabbed by a drunk.

ANDREW JOHNSON

During the period of his impeachment, the "Tennessee Tailor" found white mice in his bedroom and began leaving them handfuls of flour. "The little fellows gave me their confidence. I gave them their basket and poured some water into a bowl on the hearth for them." He was also a drunk. There is no evidence that he murdered Fido.

ULYSSES S. GRANT

Grant's horses included **Cincinnatus** (a gift from the citizens of Cincinnati), **St. Louis, Egypt, Reb, Billy Button,** and his pointedly named wartime mount, **Jeff Davis. Butcher Boy** was so fast, the President received a speeding ticket from the D.C. police.

Rosie was an unpedigreed yellow-and-black bitch.

RUTHERFORD B. HAYES

Hayes's collection of dogs included **Dot** the cocker spaniel, **Hector** the Newfoundland, **Deke** the English mastiff, **Juno** and **Shep** the hunting pups, **Grim** the greyhound (killed by a train), and **Jet** the small black mutt.

Other pets included a goat, a peacock, a cat named **Piccolomini**, and a mockingbird.

And of course there was **Miss Pussy** the Siamese cat.

JAMES GARFIELD

Veto the dog was named as a threat to Congress.

CHESTER ALAN ARTHUR

"Elegant Arthur" burned all his papers the day before he left office, and we know nothing about his pet status.*

GROVER CLEVELAND

First Lady Frances Folsom's mockingbird sang very loudly, much to the annoyance of the family's Japanese poodle and dalmatian.

BENJAMIN HARRISON

His Whiskers the goat used to drag Harrison's three grandkids in a cart, followed by **Dash** the collie.

Mr. Reciprocity and **Mr. Protection** were the resident First Opossums.

---

* The giraffe in this book is the only other invented animal. Then again, because Arthur burned his papers, we can never know for sure that he *didn't* have a giraffe.

WILLIAM MCKINLEY

Washington Post the yellow-headed Mexican parrot used to chant, "Oh, look at all the pretty girls," to anyone who passed by his cage in the White House.

First Lady Ida named four angora kittens after news figures of the day, including **Valeriano Weyler**, the Cuban governor, and **Enrique DeLome**, the Spanish Ambassador to the U.S. After the commencement of the Spanish-American War, she had those two kittens drowned.

THEODORE ROOSEVELT

TR's six children turned the White House into a veritable zoo. Dogs included **Skip** the short-legged rat terrier, **Blackjack** the Manchester terrier, **Manchu** the black Pekingese (a gift from China's Empress Dowager Ci-Xi), **Rollo** the Saint Bernard, and **Sailor Boy** the Chesapeake retriever. **Pete** the bull terrier was banished after tearing a hole in the pants of French Ambassador Jules Jusserand.

Cats included the terrorizing **Tom Quartz** and the six-toed **Slippers**.

Emily Spinach the garter snake was named so by daughter Alice "because it was green as spinach and as thin as my Aunt Emily." Quentin once unleashed his own four snakes in an Oval Office meeting.

Archie's pony **Algonquin** famously got stuck in the White House elevator, so entranced he was with his own reflection in the mirror.

Maude the pig, **Josiah** the badger, and **Jonathan** the piebald rat shared digs with the guinea pigs, **Dr. Johnson**, **Bishop Doane**, **Fighting Bob Evans**, and **Father O'Grady**.

Baron Spreckle the hen, **Eli Yale** the macaw, and a one-legged rooster with a crutch made by the kids rounded out the collection with a hyena, a coyote, a zebra, and still others.

ALL THE PRESIDENTS' PETS

WILLIAM HOWARD TAFT

Caruso the dog was a gift from opera singing star Enrico Caruso. The dog's bark was a high-pitched tenor.

Mooly Wooly, the first cow at the White House since Andrew Johnson's time, gave unsatisfactory milk.

Pauline Wayne was the last cow ever at the White House.

(Three-time presidential loser William Jennings Bryan lost his final race in 1908. He might have had better luck had he not been such a vocal critic of evolutionary theory, which he disparagingly termed "apism.")

WOODROW WILSON

Old Ike the ram, addicted to chewing tobacco, was put out to pasture under the care of AP reporter Robert Probert.

Puffins the cat ate several of the Wilsons' songbirds.

The President who once said, "If a dog will not come to you after he has looked you in the face, you ought to go home and examine your conscience," owned two of them, **Mountain Boy** the greyhound and **Bruce** the bull terrier.

WARREN HARDING

Laddie Boy the airedale was a national figure. His fictitious correspondence with the vaudeville dog star Tiger was used to defend Harding's loyalty to dubious administration officials. After the death of Harding, America's first newspaperman turned president, 19,134 members of the Newsboys Association chipped in one penny each for the casting of a statue of Laddie Boy. It resides in the Smithsonian's Museum of American History.

CALVIN COOLIDGE

Coolidge's dogs were celebrities and treated as such. Will Rogers once said, "Well, they was feeding the dogs so much that one time it looked to me like the dogs was getting more than I

227

was . . . I come pretty near getting down on my all fours and barking to see if business wouldn't pick up with me." **Rob Roy** and **Prudence Prim** the white collies, **Paul Pry** the airedale (half brother to Laddie Boy), **Calamity Jane** the Shetland sheepdog, **Boston Beans** the bulldog, and **Palo Alto** the birddog were only some of the canine occupants.

Rebecca the raccoon found temporary companionship with **Horace** the raccoon before he took off.

Most of the following pets eventually ended up at the zoo: **Ebeneezer** the donkey, a wallaby, two lion cubs, **Enoch** the goose, an antelope, a pygmy hippo, and **Smoky** the bobcat.

HERBERT HOOVER

Hoover found **King Tut** the husky on a relief trip to Belgium during World War I. A photograph of the two together was subsequently used to warm the candidate to voters during his first run for the presidency in 1928. The White House depressed Tut, though, and he died an emotional wreck.

Patrick the huge gray-brown Irish wolfhound was the great-great-grandson of Cragwood Darragh, the most famous Irish wolfhound bred in America.

Weejie the elkhound was also huge, often mistaken for a pony.

Billy the opossum was found on the White House grounds. He turned out to be the mascot of a Hyattsville, Maryland, baseball team. Hoover reluctantly returned him and the team went on to the state championships.

FRANKLIN DELANO ROOSEVELT

Fala the Scottie was living under the name **Big Boy** in Westport, Rhode Island, before he went to the White House. He was formally renamed **Murray the Outlaw of Fala Hill**, after a Roosevelt ancestor. The President chose cotton over silk sheets so that Fala could sleep on top. He went almost everywhere with the President, though he did miss Yalta.

Fala wasn't the only dog in FDR's White House. **Winks** the Llewellyn setter once gobbled up eighteen bacon and egg breakfasts. He broke his neck after running headlong into a fence.

Meggie the Scotch terrier once bit newswoman Bess Furman on the nose.

Major the German Shepherd once ripped British PM Ramsay MacDonald's pants.

HARRY S. TRUMAN

The man who said, "If you want a friend in Washington, get a dog," had little use for them. **Feller** the cocker spaniel and **Mike** the Irish setter were sent away.

Mike the Magicat wandered onto the White House lawn. The owner was famed astrologer Jeane Dixon.

DWIGHT EISENHOWER

Supreme Allied Commander Ike enjoyed the company of **Caacie** and **Telek** the Scotties—the second a gift from his driver, Kay Summersby, whose company he also enjoyed. (The man defeated Hitler. He was entitled to anything he wanted.)

Heidi the Weimaraner was highly neurotic and left a terrible stain on the Diplomatic Room's carpet.

Squirrels were the bane of Ike's putting green. They were successfully relocated to Rock Creek Park.

A giant pig, a gift from an Indianan named Elden Holsapple (just a *great* name), was sent to live on the Eisenhower farm in Gettysburg.

Vicky the vicuna was turned into a coat for Chief of Staff Sherman Adams and all hell broke loose.

JOHN F. KENNEDY

The White House ran a letter-writing contest to find homes for **Pushinka** and **Charlie**'s pupniks. Charlie, by the way, was the nephew of Asta from the *Thin Man* movies.

Shannon the Irish cocker spaniel was a gift from Irish PM Eamon De Valera. **Wolf** the Irish wolfhound was a gift from a Dublin priest named Kennedy. **Clipper** the German shepherd was a gift from Joe Kennedy to Jackie.

Billy and **Debbie** the hamsters birthed six hamsters. Billy ate them. Then Debbie ate Billy. Then Debbie died.

Macaroni the pony was a gift from LBJ to Caroline.

LYNDON BAINES JOHNSON

As Senate majority leader, LBJ had **Little Beagle Johnson**. "It's cheaper if we all have the same monogram," he said. For a while after the dog's death, the president stored his ashes over the refrigerator.

Him and **Her** the beagles made the cover of *Life* magazine when the president picked them up by the ears. Her died after swallowing a rock. Him was run over after chasing a squirrel.

Edgar the beagle was a gift from J. Edgar Hoover.

Blanco the white collie urinated on an Alexander Calder sculpture on loan from New York's Museum of Modern Art.

Yuki the mongrel was discovered by daughter Luci at a Texas gas station on Thanksgiving. Yuki was fond of Upton Sinclair and was present for the signing of the Wholesome Meat Act. He outlived the president.

RICHARD NIXON

Checkers the Cocker Spaniel, the most famous of Nixon's dogs, was a vice-presidential dog. Rumors that he would be exhumed from his Long Island grave and reburied in Yorba Linda after the death of the president in 1994 turned out to be just rumors. (If this changes anytime soon, I'll be sure to address it in paperback.)

King Timahoe the Irish setter, **Vicky** the French poodle, and **Pasha** the Yorkshire terrier are the forgotten presidential pooches.

ALL THE PRESIDENTS' PETS

GERALD FORD

Liberty the Golden retriever was a surprise gift from White House photographer David Kennerly and provided endless enjoyment to the thirty-eighth President. One of her pups, **Jerry,** became a guide dog for the blind.

JIMMY CARTER

Grits the mutt was a gift from daughter Amy's teacher. He refused to be housebroken and once tore loose from his muzzle when a vet tried to vaccinate him during Heartworm Awareness Week. He was eventually returned to the teacher.

The "killer rabbit" vs. nutria debate continues to this day.

RONALD REAGAN

Lucky the Bouvier des Flandres sheepdog stopped by Chief of Staff Don Regan's office for doughnuts every morning and grew to over eighty pounds. Regan's nemesis Nancy Reagan was soon unable to handle him, and the dog was exiled to Santa Barbara. (Was Regan intentionally sabotaging Nancy's relationship with Lucky? I'm not a conspiracy theorist.)

Rex the King Charles spaniel lived in a lavish white clapboard doghouse with a shingle roof, red curtains, and pictures of Ron and Nancy. The house was designed by Theo Hayes, the great-great-granddaughter-in-law of President Hayes.

GEORGE H.W. BUSH

Millie Kerr the springer spaniel's memoirs outsold the President's. She was voted ugliest dog by *Washingtonian* magazine. She and **C. Fred Bush** birthed six puppies.

BILL CLINTON

Buddy the chocolate Lab's death was ruled an accident and no charges were made against seventeen-year-old Halie Ritterman, driver of the car that hit him.

Socks the cat still resides with Clinton secretary Betty Currie.

GEORGE W. BUSH

Spot the springer spaniel, son of Millie, died in February 2004.

India the cat still lives, though India refused to join the Coalition of the Willing.

Barney the Scottie currently holds office.

For further information, check out Niall Kelly's *Presidential Pets*.

Acknowledgments

My agent, PJ Mark, is a saint. He made himself available to me at every hour of every day this past year for every question, query, and crisis of confidence imaginable. I took full advantage. (Next time a little less starch on the shirts, please.) Perhaps if this book is a best-seller, he won't feel so bad about having sacrificed his personal life for it. I can't thank him enough.

My editor, Annik LaFarge, was unflagging in her support of this book. She patiently explained to this first-time author that readers appreciate something called narrative. I'm guessing she was scared at times, but she only made me feel good. Thanks also to Annik's assistant, Mario Rojas. One day he will run Crown.

Don Epstein, my manager, is a rock star—not literally, thank God, because if he were he wouldn't be so whip smart before noon. Don has made all my dreams come true. Every time he calls, it's like Ed McMahon ringing my doorbell. Thanks also to my lawyer, Peter Grant, and Alan Berger and the team at CAA. Don's assistant, Sonya Giacobbe, has been tireless in accommodating my every need.

This book would not exist without the help of my friend, the brilliant Catherine Collins. She helped rearrange the random collection of factoids crowding my skull, also known as nonsense, into a story with a beginning, middle, and end. She's the best.

Mario Correa, my oldest friend, gave the book several close reads and made invaluable contributions—Quit your job, Mario!—as did my pal Adam Felber, a hilarious man who deserves his own show pronto. Thanks also to Chris Regan, a great writer with keen insight into James Buchanan, and Dolores McMullan, who gave the book an early read.

Quentin Webb is a fantastic artist. He was able to read my mind and in some cases change it, surpassing what I imagined, all in a flash. Thanks also to Rick Shiers for giving Miss Pussy life, Dan Rembert for his cover design, and Mark McCauslin for giving this book such special attention during production.

The beautiful Madeline McIntosh and the dashing Chris Pavone (aka as the Rita Hayworth and Ali Khan of publishing) are good friends and have lent vital support throughout the last year, as have Carol Bagnoli, Shannon Brigham-Hill, Lisa Dallos, Oren Izenberg, Jim Margolis, Brian O'Brien, Jeanne Simpson, and Elissa and Frank Sommerfield, Sr.

Robert Schiff, Haverford's BMOC, is a terrific guy, a fantastic researcher, and an expert anagrammatist. (That's actually a word.) He's now the go-to man on turkey buzzards.

UVA's Larry Sabato is a great professor—and funny, too. If you ever want a good five minutes on the Alien and Sedition Acts, he's the guy to call. You'll be rolling. His staff at the Center for Politics—Joshua Scott, Molly Clancy, Damon Irby, and Matt Smyth—generously gave their time to research and critique the manuscript. (I still want that tour of Zachary Taylor's birthsite.) Thanks also to interns Sarah Davis and Jenny Goodlatte.

Brooks Jackson, formerly of the AP and CNN, recounted for me the story of President Carter and the killer rabbit, which some believe to actually be a nutria.

All the agents at Greater Talent Network are friendly, fun, and very attractive. Until I met them I had no idea that mentoring college students could be so profitable.

A number of people have, at their own risk, given me platforms for appearing on camera. First and foremost, I must thank the amazing Jon Stewart and *The Daily Show*'s cocreator Madeleine Smithberg. Thanks also to NBC's Katie Couric, Matt Lauer, and Tom Touchet, MSNBC's Keith Olbermann, Fox News' Tony Snow, CNN's Jeff Greenfield, and The King, Larry King.

My friend Stephanie Simpson gave me my first job in television, on the PBS show *Wishbone*. (She opened my eyes to the creative potential in dogs.) She is a genius writer and show creator.

Dr. Stephen Ochs was my high school history teacher and continues to teach. He made a great impression on me. I'm hoping he doesn't feel like Dr. Frankenstein after reading this book.

I must thank those chroniclers that have come before me in the field of presidential pets, some of whom are mentioned in the text of this book. If I ever get to chair a Department of Presidential Pet Studies, I'm hiring all of you for my faculty.

I could not have written this book if Helen Thomas had never been born. She is a great asset to the profession of journalism, an indefatigable pursuer of truth, and an amazing character in this book. I thank her for her example. And I thank her for her love.

This book would have been impossible without the support of Frank Sommerfield. Every time I was about to jump, he pulled me back from the brink with his mumbo-jumbo therapy. He now knows more about cable news than he ever cared to know.

My brothers, Francis and Lawrence, have taught me, protected me, and backed me in every thing I've done. (Well, maybe not *everything*. They're not crazy.) I thank them in advance for supporting all my future endeavors.

You can't choose your parents—science hasn't come *that* far—so life is still something of a lottery. That's why I know I won the jackpot with my father and mother. My parents have taken as much joy in my life and career as I have. Sharing my experiences with them has made those experiences all the sweeter. (Who would have thought an appearance on CNBC's *Bullseye* could be described as "sweet"?) They have sacrificed so much for me, and I am in awe of them.

Photography Credits

Page *8*: AP/Wide World Photo

Page *39*: Picture History

Page *40*: Library of Congress, Prints and Photographs Division, reproduction number, LC-USZ62-118058

Page *41*: Library of Congress, Prints and Photographs Division, reproduction number, LC-USZ62-11417

Page *81*: Robert Knudsen, White House/John F Kennedy Library, Boston

Page *135*: Library of Congress, Prints and Photographs Division, reproduction number, LC-USZ62-17184

Page *136*: Library of Congress, Prints and Photographs Division, reproduction number, LC-USZ62-131302

Page *142*: Courtesy of Lyndon Baines Johnson Library Museum

Page *143*: Courtesy of Lyndon Baines Johnson Library Museum

Page *159*: CORBIS

Page *164*: Library of Congress, Prints and Photographs Division, reproduction number, LC-USZ62-131900

Page *166*: AP/Wide World Photo

Page *170*: Courtesy of Franklin D. Roosevelt Library

Index

TO FACILITATE THE WASHINGTON READ

Italicized page numbers indicate pictures
Parenthetic names indicate pet's owner

Index

INDEX

Index

INDEX

Index

About the Author

MO ROCCA is best known for his work on Comedy Central's *The Daily Show with Jon Stewart*. He appears frequently on NBC's *Today Show*, CNN's *Larry King Live*, MSNBC, Fox News, NPR's *Wait Wait Don't Tell Me*, and VH1. He lives in New York City.